Women in Public and Private Law Enforcement

Women in Public and Private Law Enforcement

Kathryn E. Scarborough
and
Pamela A. Collins

BUTTERWORTH
HEINEMANN

Boston   Oxford   Auckland   Johannesburg   Melbourne   New Delhi

Copyright © 2002 by Butterworth–Heinemann

ℛ A member of the Reed Elsevier group

All rights reserved.

∞ Recognizing the importance of preserving what has been written, Butterworth–Heinemann prints its books on acid-free paper whenever possible.

Library of Congress Cataloging-in-Publication Data

Scarborough, Kathryn E.
    Women in public and private law enforcement / Kathryn E.
Scarborough, Pamela A. Collins.
      p. cm.
    Includes bibliographical references and index.
    ISBN 0-7506-7115-7 (pbk. : alk. paper)
    1. Policewomen. 2. Policewomen—United States. 3. Police, Private.
4. Police, Private—United States. I. Collins, Pamela A. (Pamela Ann), 1957–
II. Title.
HV8023 .S27   2001
363.2′3′0820973—dc21

                                      2001037770

British Library Cataloguing-in-Publication Data
A catalogue record for this book is available from the British Library.

The publisher offers special discounts on bulk orders of this book.
For information, please contact:
Manager of Special Sales
Butterworth–Heinemann
225 Wildwood Avenue
Woburn, MA 01801-2041
Tel: 781-904-2500
Fax: 781-904-2620

For information on all Butterworth–Heinemann publications available,
contact our World Wide Web home page at: www.bh.com

10 9 8 7 6 5 4 3 2 1

Printed in the United States of America

Contents

Preface

Women in nontraditional occupations have been the subject of several works in sociology, psychology, business, and management. They have been studied in a variety of ways, using techniques such as participant observation or survey research. Comparisons have been made between occupations, not only for women but for men as well. Law enforcement, primarily municipal policing, has been the subject of some of these works. Heretofore, private security as law enforcement has been given scant attention. Through this book we hope to provide a comprehensive examination of women in law enforcement. By law enforcement we mean both public and private sectors, that is policing and private security. For policing, this includes not only municipal policing but also state and federal law enforcement. For security, this includes not only private security guards but also various other occupations that may be included under this rubric such as protection specialists. Due to the similar nature of these occupations we draw some comparisons that we feel are beneficial and provide further insight into the dynamics for women in these organizations. Simultaneously, we define differences when we are able, to provide an understanding of the importance of specificity with regard to this occupational analysis.

Our efforts are focused primarily on gender, with limited attention paid to race and ethnicity. Some comparisons are made when appropriate, but it is our intent to provide the most comprehensive analysis as we can with respect to gender. We feel that because of the nature of this undertaking, the reader will be better served in this capacity.

This book is intended for academicians and students of sociology, criminal justice, psychology, business, management, and loss prevention as a resource on women in nontraditional occupations, specifically law enforcement. It is also intended for professionals in the field today, to apprise them of contemporary issues for women in law enforcement, and to guide policy and procedure development. We hope this will be useful to career counselors or to those who are considering a career in law enforcement. Finally, and most importantly, it is our desire that women in law enforcement today will find this to be a work that describes how far they have come, the struggles they have faced, the challenges they have overcome, and the achievements they have made.

We draw on our experiences as a former municipal police officer and an industrial security specialist to examine this from a more practical perspective. We also approach this exploration from our chosen fields of study, in which we have obtained advanced degrees and currently work. Ours is a complementary approach, emphasizing both the importance of understanding the professions from a practical standpoint, while at the same time giving credence to academic analysis.

This text on women in law enforcement, policing, and private security describes women's entrance into these two professions and chronicles their progression. Chapter 1 provides an overview of the current status of women in policing and private security and a discussion of women in nontraditional occupations. Proposed explanations for women's limited representation are presented using theoretical frameworks identified for examining women in nontraditional, male-dominated occupations. Chapter 2 provides a historical perspective on the introduction and advancement of women in law enforcement. This chapter also contains an overview of the legal mandates that have directly impacted women's opportunities in these professions. Chapters 3 and 4 provide detailed descriptions of careers in policing and private security with gender representation when available. Chapter 5 provides a review of the research that has been done on women in policing and private security, with a major focus on women in municipal policing. This chapter focuses on attitudinal research, competency evaluations, stress, and legal issues. In Chapter 6, an overview of women executives generally is presented, with limited information on executives in municipal policing and private security. Chapter 7 presents selected issues relevant to women in contemporary law enforcement. Special attention is given to the current status of women in the workplace; the importance of mentoring and networking for women and what is known about their impact on career advancement; and community-oriented policing and women. Chapter 8 is a brief synopsis of women in policing and security internationally. The status of women internationally, contemporary research, and international women's law enforcement organizations are the focus of this chapter. The final chapter, entitled "Women Speak Out," was developed from telephone interviews of women in law enforcement today. This chapter provides the reader with a demographic overview of the respondents as well as excerpts from the interviews regarding their career choice, barriers or obstacles they have faced throughout their career, significant changes that have taken place in their profession over time, and mentoring.

Acknowledgments

An undertaking such as this requires the efforts of many people. Throughout this project we have depended on several individuals who have provided us with both personal and professional support. We sincerely appreciate the countless hours and time and energy that all have given us to enable us to complete this work.

We would like to thank Laurel Connors, Whitney Mays, and Evelyn Mynes for their assistance in research, editing, and clerical support. To Jennifer Packard and Maura Kelly, of Butterworth–Heinemann, we would like to express our sincere thanks for your persistence, patience, and encouragement. Finally, we would like to thank Jan Mays, our administrative assistant and friend: without her keeping us on the right track, helping us maintain perspective, and making us laugh when we would rather cry, we never would have completed this book. We are forever indebted to you and your efforts will not be forgotten.

Kay Scarborough would like to thank her father, Mike, who served as her inspiration while writing this book. He showed her, through example, how valuable a good work ethic is, and how important it is to consistently examine the world from others' viewpoints. She would also like to thank her great aunt Margaret Hitt, who made her believe she could be president of the United States when she was only 7 years old. Finally, and most importantly, she would like to thank K.C., her raison d'être.

Pam Collins would like to thank her mother and father, Seba and Ernest Collins, for their continued love and support, for never seeing any difference between her and her brother, and for never saying that little girls had to settle for anything less than boys. She would also like to thank Scout, her faithful companion, for her playfulness and encouragement.

Introduction

I

WOMEN'S REPRESENTATION IN LAW ENFORCEMENT

Attempting to present an accurate picture of women employed in law enforcement in the United States today is difficult at best. Not only are there numerous types of agencies, both public law enforcement and private security, but these agencies may have little or no employment information with respect to gender representation. In public law enforcement, most employee information is readily available for medium to large organizations from the Bureau of Justice Statistics, but this data does not adequately reflect small or rural organizations. Because public law enforcement agencies vary according to jurisdiction, each type of organization (such as federal, state, and local) maintains its own employee data. Additional employment information for public law enforcement officers is available through professional organization membership lists, as well as from random survey sampling.

Both the National Center for Women and Policing (NCWP) and the International Association of Chiefs of Police (IACP) have recently conducted national surveys examining women in public law enforcement. The National Center for Women and Policing surveyed 180 of the largest organizations in the United States, with a response from 126 of the organizations (70%). The organizations ranged in size from 32 employees in the Howard County Sheriff's Department in Maryland (9.4% women officers), to 12,604 employees in the Chicago Police Department (21.9% women officers) (NCWP, 2000). The International Association of Chiefs of Police in collaboration with the Gallup Organization surveyed 800 IACP members representing agencies of all sizes, with 35% of the agencies employing less than 21 officers, 39% of the agencies employing between 21 and 50 officers, and 26% of the agencies employing 51 or more officers. Seventeen percent of the agencies had no women officers, 55% had between one and four women officers, and 10% had 11 or more officers (IACP, 1998: 4).

Women comprise over half of the United States population, and a majority of the working population (outside the home). Yet recent research indicates that women in public law enforcement in large departments, which have historically provided the most opportunities for women, constitute only 14.3% of total public law enforcement (NCWP, 2000). Furthermore, recent survey research indicates that executive women in public law enforcement constitute only 7.4% (IACP, 1998). It cannot be assumed that the remaining percentage of working women would aspire to careers in law enforcement, but research has indicated that women have faced, and continue to face, barriers that prevent or discourage their pursuing law enforcement careers. Additionally, these barriers prevent women from *remaining* employed in law enforcement organizations once they have been hired.

Availability of information for private security is primarily limited to Bureau of Labor Statistics data or that obtained from professional organization memberships, such as the American Society for Industrial Security (ASIS) whose membership is currently 32,000 with approximately 1,500 being women (4.6%). According to the Bureau of Labor Statistics, women in protective services, which includes both public and private law enforcement, constituted only 15.7% of the total population. A recent survey of women in private security by the ASIS Foundation, the Women in Security Management report, identified 340 female ASIS members, with a 66.7%

response rate. Members were questioned regarding their attitudes toward their careers in security management, and nearly 75% of the respondents indicated that they were satisfied with their career choice in spite of barriers in the workplace.

Although the apparent complexities of determining the total number of women in these occupations has its limitations, it is possible to provide approximate representations, which may sometimes serve only as generalizations. Consistencies may be seen between sources of information, thereby supporting these estimates. Due to the lack of, or difficulty in, collecting data, it becomes apparent that an enormous challenge for researchers in the next century is to develop and systematically implement data collection mechanisms that provide complete information on gender representation in law enforcement, both policing and private security.

PROPOSED EXPLANATIONS FOR LOW REPRESENTATION OF WOMEN

Although women have been employed in both policing and private security for over a century, problems still exist in recruiting women to these occupations and then retaining them once they are hired. In the recent research by the NCWP and the IACP, certain issues were identified as significantly affecting the numbers of women in law enforcement. Issues included biased entry tests, discrimination, sexual harassment, lack of mentoring programs, targeted recruitment (to men), and outdated models of policing (IACP, 1998; NCWP, 2000). Earlier research has indicated that some of these issues have been historically problematic as well (Martin, 1980; Martin, 1991; Hale and Menitti, 1993).

A similar concern was raised by Women into Security Employment (WISE), a project funded by the European Social Fund Employment Target Group to encourage women wishing to return to work to consider the security industry. WISE posed the following questions:

Why, with over 18,000 vacancies in security, are not more women choosing this profession?

Why are so few women attending major conferences such as SECUREX or ASIS?

Why are so few security businesses run by women?

What are the attitudes toward women working in security?

Are there any barriers, or is it that women just are not aware of the opportunities?

(Web Site: www.ssrgroup.com, "Calling All Women—Who Me?" 5/22/99, page 1–2).

These issues, some of which are programmatic, could be effectively dealt with by policy modification or program development. However, underlying factors, which may not be as easily identified, apparently contribute to the significance of these issues and women's low representation in law enforcement occupations. Specifically, gender role expectations, the perception of law enforcement as a traditionally masculine occupation, and the existence of an exclusive occupational subculture work together to hinder women's acceptance into the men's club of law enforcement (Fletcher, 1995).

Theoretical Framework

When examining the limited numbers of women in law enforcement, it is imperative to use a multilevel approach, one that looks at the effect of society, the organization, and the individual. In the broadest sense, society shapes what we do both in organizations and as individuals, but there also exist certain characteristics specific to law enforcement organizations, which affect opportunities for individuals who may not be considered appropriate for these jobs. Furthermore, the organization may perpetuate certain individual attitudes and behaviors that do not exist in other types of organizations, because of the nature of the work, and that may also affect opportunities for certain individuals.

Cultural: Gender Roles/Gender Labeling

Appropriate gender roles are dictated by societal norms and generate expectations as to what is appropriate behavior for women and men. Expectations influence everything we do, from our choices of clothing to our choices of occupations. The magnitude of the influence of gender role expectations on individuals cannot be underestimated. Individuals are expected to conform to appropriate gender roles; when gender role expectations are violated, consequences may be minimal to severe, depending on the circumstances.

We learn what is appropriate behavior through the process of socialization, which begins shortly after birth. In fact, prior to birth, societal expectations dictate our gender roles. For example, gender appropriate names are selected by parents prior to a child's arrival. Gifts for newborns are associated with colors that are gender appropriate, with pink being designated for little girls and blue for little boys. This process is continued with the types of toys we buy our children. Little girls are given toys that are associated with gender-appropriate activity for them, such as mothering.

Socialization continues through our entire lives and permeates everything we do. When we enter the world of work, we are occupationally socialized. Through occupational socialization we learn organizational norms, beliefs, assumptions, required behavior, which are all parts of the occupational culture (Hale and Bennett, 1995). Occupations may also have subcultures, which are more distinct than the occupational cultures and which have characteristics that distinctly set them apart from others. Law enforcement subcultures have been characterized as very distinct, due to the nature of the work that sets them apart from most other occupations.

Most people spend a majority of their lives working; therefore, our work constitutes a large part of who we are as individuals. Our identities as workers sometimes supercede our personal identities, and in some instances, our identities as workers conflict with our personal identities.

Occupations are designated as appropriate for women or men based on gender roles, and labeled as such (Epstein, 1988). Consequently, those occupations that are labeled as masculine occupations are considered nontraditional for women. The more one strays from a gender-appropriate occupation, the more severe the consequences may be.

Women in Nontraditional Occupations

Studies examining women employed in nontraditional jobs frequently focus on sex-role expectations. Historically, it has been suggested that women reflect the stereotypical feminine characteristics of being weak, passive, and nurturing. These characteristics are frequently associated with women to exclude them from nontraditional employment opportunities, often segregating them into less lucrative and prestigious positions (Stromberg and Harkess, 1988). As women continue to gain entrance into nontraditional occupations, these sex-role expectations may affect opportunities and retention. To succeed, they must justify their existence in the organization, and have unusually strong reasons for their choice of careers.

Hughes (1944) proposes that status within occupations often poses a dilemma for those who do not appear to meet expectations with regards to a gender-appropriate occupation. Status is determined by characteristics that individuals possess, which may be both innate or acquired through means such as training or achievement, and the particular personal attributes proper to each status are woven into a whole (Hughes, 1944: 353). Certain characteristics, however, in the quest for achievement, may be more evident in individuals and stand out, drawing attention to the individual. In this instance, confusion, contradictions, and dilemmas of status may arise (Hughes, 1944). Hughes' description is particularly applicable to women in nontraditional occupations.

Some of these combinations of characteristics that occur seem more natural than others (Hughes, 1944). Hence, stereotyping occurs, and women are viewed as more appropriately suited to occupations that apparently require them to utilize their feminine characteristics, such as teaching or nursing. Hughes indicates that these stereotypes are composed of combinations of auxiliary characteristics, which he asserts do not necessarily correspond to the facts (Hughes, 1944: 355). Specifically, regarding occupational status, expectations concerning appropriate auxiliary characteristics are embedded in a group's views and behavior. These, then, become the group's definition of their common interests, informal code, and selection of those who become the members of the inner fraternity of the organization (Hughes, 1944: 355).

Hughes asserts that new people, who may be women in a traditionally male-dominated occupation, often challenge the solidarity of the group (Hughes, 1944: 355–356) and cause those who are already accepted group members to act adversely toward those who have not been accepted into the inner fraternity. When new people appear in organizations, sometimes status contradictions or dilemmas occur. One way of reducing status conflict is to keep the relationships among coworkers formal and specific; this could mean exclusion from the occupational subculture that, in law enforcement organizations, can be detrimental to an individual's career. Hughes identifies other means of dealing with status dilemmas in the organizations, such as shunning contact with new people, or putting them in places in which they are not so visible to the public.

Collins (1991: 11) furthers Hughes' conceptualization of a new person with the outsider-within perspective. She identifies women as marginalized by their status but indicates that this gives them a unique perspective with which to see the organization. She proposes that because of their outsider-within status, women have a distinct perspective that is different from that of the dominant group, who are men. Although the dominant group has the power to suppress the knowledge gained by the subordinate group, the subordinate group can use their outsider-within status creatively, as a source of insight and ideas (Collins, 1991: 233) with which to function in the organization. As Martin (1980) also indicates, women in policing often choose whether to emphasize a woman role, or a police role. Collins (1991) asserts, then, that some women choose to dichotomize their behavior and become two different people (p. 233). For some women, she says, playing two different roles is very difficult. For others, however, the dual roles enable them to make substantial contributions, but usually not without cost (Collins, 1991).

Women in nontraditional occupations personify the outsider-within perspective. Cultural elements precede these women prior to their entrance, with general societal expectations of what is appropriately feminine. Women in law enforcement face even more dilemmas, with the unique subcultures of the organizations and the inherently masculine orientation of the profession. Although much of what is known about women in law enforcement occupations is about women in policing and not private security, there is reason to speculate that many of the phenomena such as negative attitudes of coworkers, exist in private security as well.

Law Enforcement as a Masculine Occupation

Maleness is an essential characteristic for those in criminal justice occupations, and even more so in law enforcement. Accordingly, women would not be appropriate for these occupations because they lack one of its most primary attributes. If a woman is inappropriate for an occupation, then she is more likely perceived as incompetent or inadequate. According to Morris (1987), the fact that women are statistically rare in criminal justice occupations reaffirms perceptions of inadequacy.

Women started to work in criminal justice occupations primarily as volunteers, who were seen as extensions of their appropriate gender roles as mothers or within the scope of traditional family duties. Over the course of time, duties evolved into clerical administration, still keeping women away from what was, and still is today, considered real police work.

ORGANIZATIONAL CHARACTERISTICS

Nature of Police Work/Subculture

Policing by nature is a very closed occupation. Powers of arrest, the authority to carry a firearm, the sanctioned use of deadly force, and the inherent danger of the work contribute to the we/they mentality that is so prevalent among officers. This is an occupation that is characterized by violence, requisite physical strength, authoritarianism, and control, with a subculture that significantly affects everything within the organization. Officers are compelled to maintain solidarity in order to be successful and, at times, in order to survive. Since males have dominated the occupation since its beginning, both in numbers and in decision-making positions, it logically follows that women have had difficulty being accepted into the organization, but more specifically into its elusive subculture. When one is excluded from the subculture and on the periphery, both formal and informal assistance from coworkers or superiors may be extremely limited.

What this means, practically speaking, is that the outsider-within perspective is exemplified, leaving women, and those men who do not meet the criteria for inclusion, to fend for themselves and somehow adapt to their environment. A lack of formal assistance may be seen when a supervisor ignores a complaint by a woman officer and refuses to take action. A lack of informal assistance from a coworker may be seen when one does not share promotional information with others, making it difficult for members lacking the information to have equal opportunity for advancement. These actions may be detrimental to individuals, especially if they occur consistently and over time.

Tokenism

What goes on in the larger organization as a whole has an effect on those who are marginalized or on the periphery. It is imperative to understand both individual and organizational dynamics to get the most complete picture of those who are not readily accepted into the group. Kanter (1977) examined women and men in a large corporation and found that it is essential to not only examine individual-level variables when attempting to account for inequity, but a thorough systemic evaluation must also be undertaken. It is not only the acts of individuals within organizations that provide or prohibit opportunities. It is also the manner in which the organization operates and the opportunities, or lack thereof, that the organization perpetuates. Kanter (1977) proposes that there are three primary variables for assessing individual performance in organizations: power, opportunity, and numbers. These variables working individually or in combination constrain and shape possibilities for action and press people to adapt to their situation in a number of ways, depending on the individual, and the means available to achieve a sense of dignity (Martin, 1980: 12–13).

Power consists of the resources to get things done, the formal and informal ability to make and enforce decisions. Power is possessed by those in the dominant group in an organization. *Opportunity* means the chance for upward mobility; only jobs in the upper hierarchy offer the real power to make decisions that affect organizational policies. *Numbers* refers to the representation of certain groups of individuals, such as by gender, physical ability, or race and ethnicity. *Tokens* are those who constitute a numerical minority, which is identified as less than 15%. Kanter (1977) indicates that tokens are pressured to conform to the stereotypical images of their social group.

She identified three consequences of token status: visibility, contrast, and assimilation. She explains that as individuals of token status represent a smaller numerical proportion of the overall group, they each potentially capture a larger share of the awareness given to that group (Kanter, 1977: 210). As the group moves from skewed to tilted, in other words, increasing in numerical representation, the tokens become less individually noticed. Contrast or exaggeration of differences has more to do with the dominant group's perception of itself than it does with others' perceptions of tokens. Dominants, in attempts to preserve their commonalities, try to keep the token slightly outside, to offer a boundary for themselves (Kanter, 1977: 211) and to keep tokens in their place. Assimilation uses stereotyping to fit what are perceived generalizations about tokens. Tokens, then, have an identity to conform to immediately that is based on stereotypes about them. Kanter (1977: 211) concludes that tokens are, ironically, both highly visible as people who are different and yet not permitted the individuality of their own unique, nonstereotypical characteristics. In these instances, individual phenomena are contributing to organizational dynamics.

Kanter (1977) found that such women serve as symbols of their category, especially when they fumble, yet they also are seen as unusual examples of their kind, especially when they succeed (p. 239). This double-bind situation may create additional stress and pressure, a result that leads Kanter to conclude that tokenism is generally more harmful than beneficial.

While Kanter's work began a wave of research that more closely examined women's positions in organizations, critics claim that her work does not adequately explain the multiple complexities associated with being a woman in a traditionally masculine occupation (Yoder, 1991). Yoder claims that one's gender has an additional effect on one's token status in an occupation that is considered gender inappropriate for that individual. More specifically, men working in nontraditional occupations for men may not experience the negative effects of discrimination that women in comparable positions may experience. In fact, token status may work to men's advantages in giving them more opportunities for promotion (Yoder, 1991).

Furthermore, additional examination of occupational appropriateness and gender is necessary for a comprehensive examination of the organizational aspects that influence women's positions and participations in organizations. Yoder indicates that it is necessary to identify the importance of both gender status and occupational appropriateness in these examinations to determine whether or not women in occupations considered appropriate for women have different experiences than those considered inappropriate for women. Research should include studies that systematically vary the gender of the worker, the gender appropriateness of the occupation, and the workplace gender ratio, to tease out which factor creates which effects (p. 184).

Research that has examined Kanter's (1977) hypothesis has only looked at women and men as tokens in occupations that were considered gender inappropriate for the individuals studied. Consequently, it appears that her work is assumed to be applicable only to gender-inappropriate occupations (Yoder, 1991).

Ott (1989), in her examination of women in policing and of men in nursing, examined Kanter's hypothesis and found that males did not report the same negative effects of token status as did women in comparable positions. Even in skewed groups, men seemed to fare better than women (see Wertsch, 1998).

Individual

Martin (1997) succinctly summarizes men's individual attitudes toward women in policing. She contends that men most often object to women in policing by using their physical differences to cause concern about their inability to provide for safety and control violence. However, she points out that much more is at stake: men's perceptions are that women threaten to disrupt the division of labor, the work norms, the work group's solidarity, the insecure occupational status and public image, and the sexist ideology that undergirds the men's definition of the work as men's work and their identity as masculine men (Martin, 1997: 371). In her research on women Marines, Williams (1989) similarly indicates that these women are constantly exposed to the message that they are not men and are less capable for that (p. xiii).

Although women have proven to do their jobs as competent and effective police officers, Balkin (1988) indicates that policemen still do not like policewomen even if they have worked directly with them. The reasons for this, he contends, are both cultural and interpersonal. When discussing cultural explanations he indicates that attitudes are a result of values about sex roles and work. Balkin (1988: 35) states that policemen have learned traditional values and held onto them, making them very unreceptive to women in policing. As stated previously, women also threaten the solidarity of the policemen, which has a significant effect on the perception of isolation from the public as well as the dangerousness of their jobs.

From a strictly personal perspective, Balkin (1988) proposes that some men may enter policing to overcome disappointment from their parents for not being manly enough. Police work exemplifies what is manly through the characterization of the job as requiring strength, aggression, bravery, and superiority to women (p. 36). This job encourages a man to exhibit the qualities that make him feel manly and thus maintain his security (p. 36). However, if a woman can be allowed to perform police work *and* performs effectively, this threatens his masculinity. Hence, the negative attitudes still persist. Balkin (1988) further indicates that the presence of women in policing causes men in policing anxiety. Horne (1980), Martin (1980), and Wexler and Logan (1983) also indicate that women in policing threaten their counterparts' masculinity.

It is apparent that any theoretical explanation for the status of women in law enforcement is complex and relies on a multidimensional approach. What has been offered as explanation has been supported in large part by research that primarily examines women in policing.

Before their entrance into uniform patrol, women's participation in law enforcement organizations was confined to those tasks that appeared suitable based on what society prescribes as feminine through gender labeling. The women's movement, the due process revolution, case law, and legislation removed some barriers for women, allowing them to become more active in law enforcement organizations. In most cases, organizations were forced into allowing women equal opportunities. Although the legal mandates exist and may be enforced, these may do nothing to affect the organizational culture or attitudes toward women in the organization. What follows in Chapter 2 is a chronology of women in law enforcement, primarily policing, and a historical analysis of the legal and social factors that have contributed to women's participation in law enforcement, or the lack thereof.

2

History and Legal Mandates

The recorded history of women in law enforcement has primarily chronicled women in the public sector. The history of private security has developed in large part without noting the presence of women in the profession. Most of this chapter consists of the history of women in policing. However, the evolution of legal mandates has affected women in all occupations and is discussed accordingly.

WOMEN'S PARTICIPATION IN PUBLIC LAW ENFORCEMENT

Schulz (1995a) divides the history of women in policing into six eras as described in the chapters in her book: (1) Forerunners: The Matrons, 1820–1899; (2) The Early Policewomen, 1900–1928; (3) Depression Losses, 1929–1941; (4) World War II and the 1940s; (5) Paving the Way for Patrol, 1950–1967; and (6) Women Become Crimefighters, 1968—The Present. She describes the evolution of women in policing and "how initial demands for a limited, specialized role based on gender were replaced by demands for equality by later generations of women with totally different social histories and self images" (Schulz, 1995a: 1). The former social matron of

15

policing has been superceded over time with the woman in a "unisex role" with male coworkers (Schulz, 1995a: 1).

The forerunners of women in policing spent their time performing matronly or maternal activities, generally associated with women and children. Women's participation in policing ran parallel to their roles as jail and prison matrons. Women's presence in these occupations was greatly affected by temperance leaders, social purity crusaders, and women social reformers. Much of the impetus driving women into these occupations was provided by these social leaders who felt it was necessary to save fallen women in prison and deal with women and children in police custody.

HISTORY

Women's employment in law enforcement occupations is best documented by beginning in the mid- to late-nineteenth century. During this time, women were spies, undercover agents, and detectives in prominent organizations such as the Pinkerton Detective Agency and Wells Fargo (More, 1998). Much of the increased participation of women in law enforcement ran parallel to the social movements in both the United States and Great Britain. Reformers advocated women's participation in law enforcement organizations not only to deal with women prisoners, women victims, and juveniles, but also to help change police practices.

In 1845, prior to the American Civil War, New York City hired its first jail matron, as a result of pressure from the American Female Society (More, 1998). Roughly thirty years later, in 1888, both New York and Massachusetts made it mandatory for communities with populations over 20,000 to hire women to care for women prisoners (Horne, 1980: 17). In 1893, Marie Owens was the first woman to be appointed as a police officer, without powers of arrest, by the Mayor of Chicago. In 1905, Lola Baldwin was designated as a "safety worker" with powers of arrest who was tasked with looking after women and children at the Lewis and Clark Exposition in Portland, Oregon. During the same year, Portland also became the first city in the United States to organize a Women's Bureau in its police department (Lunnenborg, 1989). In 1910, the first woman sworn into public law enforcement in the United States, with powers of arrest, was Alice Stebbins Wells. She was given the title of woman police officer (Lunnenborg, 1989; Schulz, 1995a).

Wells was a student of theology and social work who garnered a lot of attention through her activism and soon became a "prime mover" in the policewomen's movement (More, 1998: 196). She had the support of reform organizations and was able to effectively channel efforts to support her cause. Her notoriety enabled her to assist in the creation of the International Association of Policewomen, which was the first organization solely devoted to supporting women in policing. This organization has undergone many changes since Wells' tenure, but would likely not have been successful without her involvement early on.

In the 1920s, during a time in American policing in which there was a drive to professionalize the organization, August Vollmer, Berkeley, California, Chief of Police, appointed Elizabeth G. Lossing to supervise a newly established crime prevention unit in this department (More, 1998). Lossing, a highly educated woman for her day with a B.S. from Mills College, was tasked primarily with dealing with juvenile delinquency problems, which is not surprising given the notion of the effectiveness of women in dealing with other women and children and their relegation to such duties. It is notable, however, that even at this point in time, Lossing was tasked with involving other agencies to address the problem of juvenile delinquency (More, 1998). This approach is community-oriented and one that is quite prevalent today.

The first known recorded employment of a woman in private law enforcement was with the Pinkerton Security Company in the late 1850s. Pinkerton is considered one of the oldest and largest private security companies in the United States. The company got its start when it began the Pinkerton Protection Patrol of private watchmen for railroad yards and industrial areas. It was the railroad security services that provided an opportunity for the first female detective to be hired.

Although women had been working in law enforcement in the nineteenth century, they were functioning as police matrons working primarily with juveniles and women. When duties for women in policing expanded in the early 1900s after they were first granted powers of arrest, much of their work was confined to supervising and enforcing laws concerning dance halls, skating rinks and theaters, monitoring billboard displays, locating missing persons, and maintaining a general information bureau for women seeking advice (Higgins, 1951; Schulz, 1995a).

In 1922 at the annual meeting of the International Association of Chiefs of Police (IACP), role distinctions between women and men were emphasized. Women were required to have a good education and formal training and experience in social work, which would make them better qualified to undertake the responsibilities of crime prevention and protection work (Hale, 1992; Hutzel, 1933; Walker, 1977). Similar or comparable requirements for men did not exist. In addition to those qualifications related to education and training, women were required to have a pleasant personality and a positive attitude in dealing with the problems of young women. They were expected to be tolerant, sympathetic, emotionally stable, and possess common sense (Hutzel, 1933). Although the IACP took this approach, the organization still passed a resolution supporting the use of women in law enforcement (More, 1998). In other words, the organization was supportive of women's involvement, but only on acceptable terms—that is, in roles considered "appropriately female."

In the 1920s and 1930s women's participation in law enforcement varied. World War I provided for the increased participation of women in law enforcement as it did in many other occupations, due to men's increased participation in military efforts. According to the Census, in 1930 there were 1,534 women in public and private law enforcement agencies, and by 1940 that number had increased to 1,775 (Schulz, 1995b). More specifically, Schulz (1995b) notes that by 1929 there were over 600 women serving in primarily large municipal police organizations throughout the United States. However, during the 1930s the number of women decreased, perhaps because of the contrasting image of the police as crimefighters that appeared at that time. Unlike the benevolent social worker, which had been exemplified by the women in policing heretofore, the crimefighting officer was a stark contrast to those whose mission it was to provide social direction and support to the community. Consequently, by 1940, there were roughly 500 policewomen in the United States. This would suggest that the increase that appeared between 1930 and 1940 occurred in private security.

With World War II, another shift occurred that brought the nation's focus back to concerns of morality and delinquency, which better fit the policewoman's image and reality. Unlike their counterparts in other areas of the labor force, policewomen at this time were not hired as temporary replacements for policemen who went to war (Schulz, 1995b). Instead, these women were hired to do exactly what they had been doing since their entrance into the world of law enforcement—performing stereotypical tasks dealing with women and children and focusing more on social work and crime prevention. After World War II, women were given different kinds of assignments, such as investigations, and were provided with better uniforms and firearms training (Schulz, 1995b), which meant that, for the first time, women were slowly breaking free from the stereotypical roles that had restricted them for so long. Schulz indicates that by 1950, there were more than 2,500 policewomen in public law enforcement, which was slightly more than 1% of the total population. It is apparent that a turning point in the history of women in law enforcement occurred during the 1950s and 1960s when women began to be used in roles other than those that dealt with other women and children.

Schulz points out that this time period was significant for policewomen not only for the availability of new opportunities, but also because "a different type of woman was brought into policing" (Schulz, 1995a: 378). The different woman was, unlike her upper-middle-class predecessors who had focused on saving society from social ills, a middle-class careerist interested in "real" police work. Described as "second generation" policewomen who entered police work to take advantage of opportunities versus trying to reform society, these women were intent on gaining professional recognition, hence the formation of the International Association of Policewomen (Schulz, 1995a). These new policewomen had a better view of the complete world of police work, which provided an impetus for them to pursue opportunities from which they had previously been excluded. The upcoming decades were a time in which women in policing fought diligently to achieve equality in all areas of policing.

Although job assignments remained relatively stable for women in the early 1960s, this shifted toward the end of the decade when women were allowed to work in uniformed patrol for the first time. In 1965, Miami utilized women in field operations, while the District of Columbia dissolved their women's bureau and began to utilize women in patrol (More, 1998). In 1968, Indianapolis, Indiana, followed suit, by not only assigning women to patrol units but by also assigning two women to patrol as partners (Schulz, 1995a). The early 1970s saw a widespread increase throughout the nation. Although the increase occurred nationally, the total numbers of women in law enforcement did not change dramatically.

Until women entered patrol work, minimal research was undertaken to evaluate the competency of women in this nontraditional occupation. The primary reason for the dearth of research can be attributed to the fact that women had been performing tasks that were considered gender appropriate. When they entered patrol, however, this necessitated their participation in situations that were identified as dangerous, requiring physical strength and dominance, neither of which women were thought to possess. Therefore, it appeared imperative to evaluate the competency of women in these positions.

Although women have worked in policing as sworn officers since 1910 (Schulz, 1995a), their participation was limited and previously confined to what were considered gender-appropriate tasks. Policing has been characterized as requiring physical strength and the ability to control potentially violent situations, which are deemed as inherently masculine characteristics. Consequently, since women are perceived as lacking these characteristics, they have been viewed as incompetent. Because of the characterization of the job as appropriate for men only and inconsistent with appropriate female activities, women have experienced discrimination in various forms throughout the tenure of their careers. A detailed synopsis of research on women in law enforcement may be found in Chapter 5.

LEGAL MANDATES

Women's participation in nontraditional occupations such as policing was profoundly changed during the 1960s and 1970s as a result of civil rights legislation, significant court cases, the women's movement, and the due process revolution. These gave women and people of color assistance that they had not previously had in addressing discriminatory practices, which had long plagued the police organization.

Harriman (1996) indicates that historically men have made employment gains through participation in the labor movement, while women have made gains as a result of legislation. However, with initial legislation that was intended to protect women and children from exploitation as workers, discrimination was actually increased. Today, legislation is aimed more at discrimination related to issues such as promotion and retention, wages, and training (Harriman, 1996).

In the nineteenth century, there was an influx of women workers into the labor force who went to work in traditionally female occupations such as seamstresses and waitresses. Working conditions for women at this time were atrocious and much worse for women than for men. As time went on conditions worsened for women while disparities between women and men increased. Significantly, when conditions became bad enough for women, legislation was sought to protect them—but not men. Social reformers became active in efforts to protect women through legislation at this time (Harriman, 1996).

Hartmann (1976) indicates that because women were paid less than men, they were a threat to men's jobs. This resulted in the exclusion of women from organized efforts to better working conditions, which if protective legislation were passed would serve to keep women in their appropriate place in the home, instead of in the labor force competing with men. Harriman (1996) indicates that from 1867 to 1964, protective legislation was enacted to limit women's working hours and conditions, although most of the legislation was suspended during World War II due to worker shortages. When the war was over, the legislation and protective efforts resumed (Harriman, 1996).

The Equal Pay Act of 1963, a precursor to the Civil Rights Act of 1964, was not a "major departure from the paternalistic posture of protective legislation" as previously identified (Harriman, 1996: 49). This Act provided a limited guarantee of pay equity, but excluded comparable positions if differences were based on "a seniority system, a merit system, a system that measured earnings by quantity or quality of production, or a difference based on any other factor than sex" (Harriman, 1996: 49).

In 1964 Congress passed Title VII of the Civil Rights Act, which was designed primarily to address the problem of race discrimination. This brought some degree of relief from discriminatory practices. This legislation made it unlawful for private employers with 25 or more employees to discriminate in recruitment, hiring, working conditions, promotion, or other employment practices based on race, color, religion, sex, or national origin. In 1972, the Equal Employment Opportunity Act extended the application of Title VII to state and local governments, which included police departments. This Act also created the Equal Employment Opportunities Commission (EEOC) to oversee its enforcement.

Congress passed the Omnibus Crime Control and Safe Streets Act of 1968, which created the Law Enforcement Assistance Administration (LEAA). A significant provision of LEAA was for personnel training. LEAA monies not only made it easier for law enforcement organizations to raise educational standards, but it also provided opportunities for women and people of color to obtain degrees in fields from which they had been previously excluded. The development of LEAA, close to the time of significant legal cases, provided a more open door for women than had been seen up until that time. Furthermore, the 1968 Omnibus Crime Control Act was amended by the 1973 Crime Control Act, which prohibited discrimination against women in the employment practices of any agency receiving LEAA funds. LEAA Equal Opportunity Employment guidelines required that agencies assess recruiting, hiring, promotion, and training procedures, and develop an EEO program that had to be filed with the state planning agency. The guidelines also mandated that agencies insure that hiring standards demonstrate job-relatedness in order to prevent discrimination. Agencies that did not comply were subject to withholding of LEAA funds.

The Pregnancy Discrimination Act of 1978 prohibited discrimination on the basis of pregnancy, childbirth, or related medical conditions and required employers to treat these conditions as any other temporary disability with regards to benefits. It allowed employers to provide additional protection for pregnant workers, but it did not require them to do so.

This various legislation provided the impetus for allowing women in uniform to patrol in the late 1960s and early 1970s. Prior to this, women were exclusively performing gender-appropriate tasks dealing with women, juveniles, or clerical support. Significant court cases, such as *Griggs v. Duke Power Co.* (1971), *Meritor Savings Bank FSB v. Vinson* (1986), and *Harris v. Forklift Systems, Inc.* (1993), also helped to clarify civil rights legislation and provided more opportunities for women's participation in policing.

In *Griggs v. Duke Power Co.* (1971), the Court held that a plaintiff does not have to prove intentional discrimination on the part of the employer. The burden of proof falls on the employer to prove that the job requirements are bona fide occupational qualifications (BFOQ), and that no other means of selection could be used, once a plaintiff proves that job qualifications exclude a certain group or class more than another. The *Griggs* standard was then used to evaluate height and weight requirements that had previously excluded women from employment in policing.

Meritor Savings Bank FSB v. Vinson (1986), clarified issues relating to sexual harassment, which were identified as problematic for women in policing (Gomez-Preston and Trescott, 1995; Hale and Menniti, 1993) and which were also a form of sex discrimination prohibited under Title VII. In *Meritor*, the Court held that both quid pro quo harassment and hostile work environment are prohibited by Title VII. The Court held that for harassment to be a cause of action in a hostile work environment, the plaintiff must suffer severe or pervasive treatment that affects the conditions of the plaintiff's employment. However, in *Harris v. Forklift Systems, Inc.* (1993), the Court ruled that a hostile work environment does not have to seriously affect a plaintiff's psychological well-being or cause injury. Instead, the Court articulated a midpoint between what is merely offensive behavior and what is psychologically detrimental to the plaintiff.

One case, although not a Supreme Court case, that had a significant impact on women in policing, especially with regards to promotion, and that exemplifies the hard battles fought to achieve equality, is *Shpritzer v. Lang* (1961). Felicia Shpritzer was a policewoman in New York City who sued to take the exam for sergeant. Schulz indicates that Shpritzer "personified the changes that began in the 1960s" (Schulz: 1995b:125).

Shpritzer was a highly educated woman with two master's degrees who had previously taught in the public schools. She waited four years to be appointed as an officer after passing the civil service exam, because there were no positions available for women at the time she passed the test. Shpritzer worked in the juvenile division at the time of the lawsuit and remained there most of her career.

She brought a class action suit on behalf of the women in the department who were not allowed to take the promotion exam. The court found in her behalf, and although the City of New York appealed the decision, the Appeals Court upheld the lower court's decision. Following the decision, 126 women of the New York City Police Department were allowed to take the promotion exam for sergeant. Shpritzer, along with her colleague, Gertrude Schimmel, had the two highest scores on the exam and were subsequently promoted to sergeant. Shpritzer and Schimmel were both promoted to lieutenant, and Shpritzer retired as one, while on the list for captain. Schimmel retired as a Deputy Chief in 1978, and at the time was commanding officer of the Office of the Deputy Commissioner, Community Affairs. Schulz (1995b: 126) indicates that in many cities, cases like this served as women's "primary path to equal opportunity."

Court cases, along with other legislation, provided for the development of affirmative action programs, which in some cases required quotas and timetables for hiring women. Affirmative action programs were intended to address the results of past discrimination.

Although women represented only 2.2% of sworn personnel in municipal police organizations in 1975, representation had increased to 9% by 1993, constituting almost a 7% gain (Martin and Jurik, 1996). By 1998, women in large police organizations constituted almost 14% (NCWP, 1999). According to a longitudinal study spanning a 30-year period, women working in private security in the St. Louis, Missouri, area, doubled from 1959 to 1989 (Cunningham, Strauchs, and Van Meter, 1990). Had it not been for civil rights legislation and other legal mandates, these increases may have never been realized.

3

Public Law Enforcement

Public law enforcement represents the first step for people entering the criminal justice system. Law enforcement officers are the primary agents for social control in the United States. These officers are more often under direct scrutiny than any other criminal justice agent, and consequently subject to higher levels of criticism. What is appropriate behavior for these officials is frequently the subject of much concern and public debate. Historically, law enforcement officers have been seen as primarily crime fighters, responding only when needed to incidents involving criminal activity, and this was considered appropriate behavior. Over the course of time, what has been deemed appropriate behavior has changed. Law enforcement today is supposed to be not only reactive, but also proactive, attempting to alleviate criminal activity before it happens. These changes represent the shift from a traditional, professional model of law enforcement to a more community-oriented model, as seen with Community Oriented Policing (COP). Although COP has been readily recognized in municipal police organizations, it can be argued that there have been changes in philosophy in many other types of law enforcement agencies, due to societal changes and public demands, and that these agencies also operate using a more community-oriented model.

What these philosophical changes mean is that the law enforcement organizations of today are much different than they were in the late 1800s when women were matrons focusing on incidents involving women and children. The situation today is also much different from the turbulent 1960s and 1970s when women first entered uniform patrol and were subject to more scrutiny than that which generally comes with the job of law enforcement. The climate is much different today than it was when Penny Harrington sued the Portland Police Department for sex discrimination in 1973 and was subsequently sworn in as the first female police chief of a large U.S. city in 1985 (Myers, 1995). At no other time in the history of women in law enforcement have there been more opportunities for women to become a part of these organizations—and to make substantial contributions—without so many of the barriers that existed in the past. What is valued in law enforcement officers of today are qualities that have been valued in women historically but have been denigrated in law enforcement.

Although some of these qualities are designated as stereotypically feminine in nature, they have been consistently observed in women more often than men. It remains to be seen how this shift in philosophy may affect the representation of women in law enforcement. This chapter includes descriptions of various occupations in federal, state, and municipal law enforcement. When available, statistics on the representation of women are presented.

The following is a gender breakdown of state and local law enforcement organizations with agencies of 100 or more officers (Reeves and Goldberg, 1999). It is important to recognize that small and rural organizations are not represented in this breakdown, and that the status of women in rural organizations is relatively unknown. (See Figure 3.1.)

The average representation of women in these organizations is 10%. In a recent study of large police organizations by the National Center for Women and Policing (see the chart in Figure 3.2), women were found to represent 16.6% in municipal organizations, 11.1% in county and sheriff's organizations, and a mere 6.2% in state police

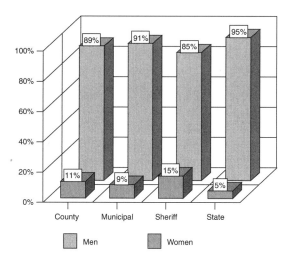

Figure 3.1. Summary data for state and local enforcement agencies with 100 or more officers, by type of agency, 1997, Bureau of Justice Statistics.

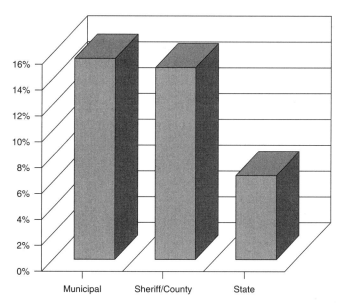

Figure 3.2. Percentage of women in local enforcement agencies. National Center for Women and Policing. *Equality Denied: The Status of Women in Policing.* Los Angeles, CA: Feminist Majority Foundation, 2000.

organizations. Data was gathered from two different sources in this case and appears to be relatively consistent.

FEDERAL, STATE, AND MUNICIPAL LAW ENFORCEMENT

Unlike private security, law enforcement careers can be divided into three levels: federal, state, and municipal or local. Organizations associated with levels of government have developed as a result of responses to specific needs of citizens (Gaines, Kappeler, and Vaughn, 1999). Within each of these levels, there are numerous agencies that provide employment opportunities for those interested in law enforcement (DeLucia and Doyle, 1998). What follows is a general description of opportunities at each level, with examples of specific positions.

Federal

In 1996, there were approximately 60 different federal law enforcement agencies with almost 75,000 employees (Gaines, Kappeler, and Vaughn, 1999). Although most federal law enforcement officers are employed in the Department of the Treasury and Justice, other federal departments have law enforcement personnel as well. Table 3.1 identifies federal agencies with 500 or more employees who are full-time officers and are authorized to carry a firearm. A gender breakdown of these organizations is included. Representation of females range from 8.2% in the U.S. Fish and Wildlife Service to 23.4% in the Internal Revenue Service. The average representation for women in federal agencies is 13.4%, which is similar to what the National Center for Women and Policing found in larger, municipal police organizations.

Beyond information about gender representation in federal agencies, there is limited available information about women employed in federal agencies. Therefore, only general descriptions of the duties of federal agencies in the previous list and others that may

Table 3.1   Federal agencies employing 500 or more full-time officers
with authority to carry firearms and make arrests, June 1996.

Agency	Number of Full-Time Federal Officers	Sex (Percentage)	
		Male	Female
Immigration and Naturalization	12,403	87.3	12.7
Federal Bureau of Prisons	11,329	87.7	12.3
Federal Bureau of Investigation	10,389	85.5	14.5
U.S. Customs Service	9,749	82.7	17.3
Internal Revenue Service	3,784	76.6	23.4
U.S. Postal Inspection Service	3,576	85.9	14.1
U.S. Secret Service	3,185	91.2	8.8
Drug Enforcement Agency	2,946	*	*
Administrative Office of the Courts	2,777	*	*
U.S. Marshals Service	2,650	88.3	11.7
National Park Service	2,148	86.2	13.8
Bureau of Alcohol, Tobacco and Firearms	1,869	88.3	11.7
U.S. Capital Police	1,031	83.2	16.8
U.S. Fish and Wildlife	869	91.8	8.2
G.S.A. B Federal Protective Service	643	90.4	9.6
U.S. Forest Service	619	84.5	15.5

not be as large as those organizations but which offer employment
opportunities are represented.

Administrative Office of the United States Courts

The primary duty of a court administrator is to assist the judge in
daily operations of the U.S. federal courts. Other duties may include
development of policies and procedures for court calendars and pro-

grams, coordinating court data processing, preparation of reports of court data, and insuring proper case disposition (DeLucia and Doyle, 1998).

Alcohol, Tobacco, and Firearms Special Agent

The primary duties of these agents include investigating federal law violations dealing with firearms or explosives, enforcing liquor and tobacco law, and assisting the Secret Service in presidential protection (DeLucia and Doyle, 1998).

United States Customs Special Agent

The primary duties of these agents include investigating criminal fraud against the U.S. revenue, countervaluing (which means to undervalue imported and exported property), cargo thefts, and illegal importation and exportation (DeLucia and Doyle, 1998).

Deputy United States Marshal

The primary duties of these agents include providing federal court security, protection of federal witnesses, investigation of federal fugitives, liaison with INTERPOL, transportation and custody of federal prisoners, and dealing with national emergencies when necessary (DeLucia and Doyle, 1998).

Drug Enforcement Special Agent

The primary duty of these agents includes attempting to stop the flow of illegal drugs throughout the country and abroad. More specific duties include criminal surveillance, undercover infiltration of drug channels, identifying and apprehending drug traffickers, confiscating illegal drug supplies, and arresting law violators engaged in criminal drug activities (DeLucia and Doyle, 1998).

Federal Bureau of Investigation Special Agent

The primary duties of these agents include dealing with kidnapping, bank robbery, organized crime, civil rights violations, fraud, and spying. FBI agents primarily concentrate on the investigation function of law enforcement and work very closely with the U.S. Attorney General (DeLucia and Doyle, 1998).

Federal Bureau of Prisons (Correctional Treatment Specialist)

The primary focus of these officers is performing correctional casework in a federal institutional setting. Duties include developing, evaluating, and analyzing program needs; evaluating individual inmate progress; and coordinating inmate training (DeLucia and Doyle, 1998).

Federal Protective Service Officer

These agents provide security for the U.S. General Services Administration (GSA), which is responsible for most civilian work space in the federal government. Primary duties of the agents include law enforcement, physical security, personnel investigation, electronic surveillance, and crime prevention (DeLucia and Doyle, 1998).

Fish and Wildlife Service Special Agent

The primary duties of these agents include investigating violations of the Federal Fish and Wildlife laws, and protecting, maintaining, controlling, and improving national fish and wildlife resources (DeLucia and Doyle, 1998).

Immigration and Naturalization Service, Border Patrol Agent

The primary duties of these agents include detecting and preventing the illegal entry of persons into the United States along the 8,000 miles of land and water that is U.S. territory (DeLucia and Doyle, 1998).

Internal Revenue Criminal Investigator

The primary duties of these agents include investigating charges of both criminal and civil violations of the Internal Revenue laws. These agents must have strong backgrounds in accounting (DeLucia and Doyle, 1998).

Naval Investigative Service/Criminal Investigator

The primary duties of these agents include conducting criminal investigations and counterintelligence for the Department of the Navy. More specific duties include the criminal investigation of arson, homicide, rape, robbery, narcotics trafficking, larceny, and destruction of government property, foreign counterintelligence, bribery, contract and check fraud, weapons theft, and antiterrorist activities (DeLucia and Doyle, 1998).

United States Park Police

The primary duty of these officers is providing law enforcement for the national parks. Additionally, park police may provide executive protection for dignitaries, both foreign and domestic, and provide assistance to other agencies in law enforcement emergencies (DeLucia and Doyle, 1998).

U.S. Postal Service Inspector

The primary duties of these inspectors include criminal and audit investigations of the United States Postal Service. Additionally, inspectors are required to perform various security and administrative duties (DeLucia and Doyle, 1998).

Secret Service Agent

The primary duties of these agents include executive protection and investigation of crimes against the currency, such as counterfeiting, and forging and cashing of government bonds, checks, and securities (DeLucia and Doyle, 1998).

State Police Organizations

State police organizations exist in every state in the United States except Hawaii. These law enforcement organizations include state police, highway patrol, department of public safety, wildlife and game commissions, and some specific organizations such as the Texas Rangers. Contrary to popular belief, state police officers or troopers do not solely provide traffic enforcement. Their duties are much broader than simply traffic enforcement. The primary duties of these officers include enforcing statewide motor vehicle and criminal laws and ensuring public safety. General tasks typically performed by these officers include providing information to motorists, assisting with disabled vehicles, identifying illegally operated vehicles, and investigating traffic accidents. State police organizations as a whole have the lowest representation of women when compared to other types of law enforcement organizations on average (DeLucia and Doyle, 1998). In a recent survey of 100 of the largest public law enforcement organizations in the United States conducted by the National Center for Women and Policing, women represented 6.2% of employees in state police organizations (NCWP, 2000). The representation of women in state police organizations in various regions of the country ranges from 4% in the Southern and Southwestern states to 8% in the New England states. As with federal law enforcement agencies, other than numerical representation very little is known about women in state police organizations. (See Table 3.2 and Figure 3.3, Reaves and Goldberg, 1999.)

Municipal Police Organizations

Municipal police officers, or those that work in cities and towns, are probably the ones most familiar to citizens. These officers have more contact with the public than any other actor in the criminal justice system. Very broadly, these officers are tasked with protecting the life and property of citizens. Organizations range in size from a single officer to over 5,000 officers in major departments. Specialization within a department depends on the size of the organization. Larger organizations would be more likely to have a Criminal Investigation Division than a smaller organization would.

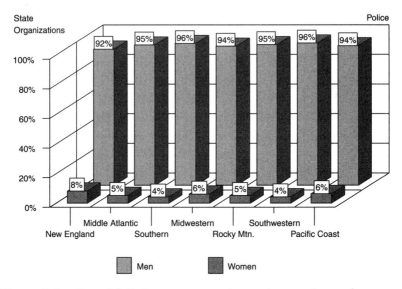

Figure 3.3. Sex of full-time sworn employees in state law enforcement agencies by region, 1997, Bureau of Justice Statistics.

Table 3.2 Breakdown of states that represent the regions shown in Figure 3.3.

New England	CT, ME, MA, NH, RI, VT
Middle Atlantic	NJ, NY, PA
Southern	AL, AR, DE, FL, GA, KY, LA, MD, MS, NC, SC, TN, VA, WV
Midwestern	IL, IN, IO, KS, MI, MN, MO, NE, ND, OH, SD, WI
Rocky Mountain	CO, ID, MT, NV, UT, WY
Southwestern	AZ, NM, OK, TX
Pacific Coast	AK, CA, OR, WA

Note: Illinois data was not provided for this table.

All municipal police organizations have uniformed patrol officers, and uniformed patrol officers comprise the largest number of officers in police organizations. These officers perform a variety of functions and are most often perceived as generalists. What this means is that uniformed patrol officers must be well versed in the multifaceted job of policing in order to perform their duties acceptably.

Local law enforcement organizations vary with size more than function and include both municipal and county organizations. Most local public law enforcement organizations are small, consisting of 20 officers or less. However, as noted earlier, much of the employment information gathered to date has been taken from medium or large departments and generalized to the entire law enforcement population. Obviously, omitting small organizations detracts from the accuracy of the data presented.

According to the most recent Bureau of Labor Statistics (BLS) data, women employed in local public law enforcement constituted 15.8% of the total population of public law enforcement (BLS, 1996). More specifically, women working as police or detectives represented 11.3%, whereas women working as sheriffs, bailiffs, and other related law enforcement represented 16.4% of the population (BLS, 1996). The National Center for Women in Policing found that women accounted for 11.1% of sheriff or county police organizations (NCWP, 2000).

An interesting comparison can be made to women in military law enforcement organizations, due to the similarities of the occupations. Women in military law enforcement occupations with powers of arrest and firearm authorization constituted from 5.9% in the U.S. Marine Corps to 16.9% in the U.S. Army Intelligence and Security Command. The average representation of women in these military organizations in 13.8%. This representation is comparable to women's representation at both the federal level and in large municipal organizations. (See Table 3.3, Reaves and Goldberg, 1999.)

There are numerous employment opportunities for women in various public law enforcement organizations associated with every level of government. As was demonstrated, women represented, at best, no more than 25% of personnel in public law enforcement organizations, with typical ranges of 10% to 12% in most organizations. Reasons for the limited representation of women

Table 3.3 Gender representation among officers with arrest and selected components of the U.S. Armed Forces, June 1996.

Army	Number of Officers	Sex	
		Male	Female
Criminal Investigation Command	580	86.7	13.3
Intelligence and Security Command	710	83.1	16.9
Military Police	1,372	83.2	16.8
U.S. Navy, Naval Investigative	897	84.7	15.3
U.S. Marine Corps	3,629	94.1	5.9

Note: This table does not represent complete data for the U.S. Armed Forces. It includes only those branches and components of the U.S. Armed Forces that responded to the BJS (Bureau of Justice Statistics) survey. Female and minority representation among officers with arrest and selected components of the U.S. Armed Forces, June 1996.

have been offered, based on research and anecdotal evidence. Questions still arise, however, regarding women's lack of representation. Chapter 5 includes a detailed examination of research that has attempted to answer some of the questions about women in law enforcement.

4

Private Security

This chapter will provide an analysis of types of occupations and the representation of women in private sector organizations. General descriptions of opportunities available in private security will be presented where available.

The best single source for identifying the gender demographics of the security professions is the American Society for Industrial Security (ASIS) membership. ASIS is the largest international organization for security professionals with a membership of approximately 32,000 members. According to ASIS the membership has a distinct profile that is described as follows:

Approximately 70% of ASIS members hold at least a bachelor's degree and 25% have a graduate degree. A little more than the majority, 55%, work in either corporate or industrial security; 13% are independent security consultants; and the rest are working as security professionals in the military or federal government, public law enforcement, equipment and contract service sales, marketing, and operations professionals. Nearly 50% of all security professionals are responsible for a departmental budget of over $1 million. Security professionals' average household income is greater than $96,000.

According to data provided by ASIS, the following describes the female representation in this organization today. Certainly this is not generalizable to women's representation in the entire profession, but it does provide a snapshot of women in security.

The chart in Figure 4.1 illustrates the range of fiscal responsibility that women in security possess. In this illustration annual security budgets range from $10,000 to $20,000,000. It would appear that the majority of the women represented in this example have annual budgets exceeding $1 million.

Figure 4.2 illustrates that the majority of women security professionals are working in organizations with 1,000 or less employees. More than 500 women security professionals indicated that they work for companies with 100 or less employees, which would indicate that this may be where the greatest opportunities for employment and promotion exist for women.

Table 4.1 provides a greater insight into the type of business or type of company in which women security professionals are employed.

Based upon Table 4.1 it would appear that the majority of women are employed in the security service sector. This could include contract security companies offering guard and investigative services, or in the security technology industry. An interesting point to consider is that women security professionals are represented

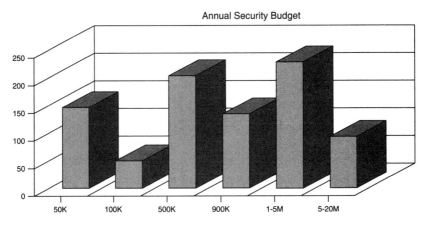

Figure 4.1.   Annual Security Budget: Company's Security Budget—Breakdown as of 11 June 1999, ASIS.

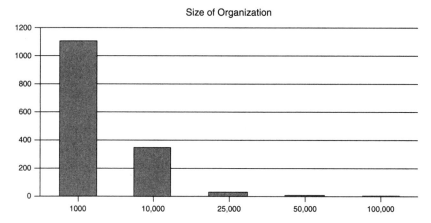

Figure 4.2.   Employees at Member's Location—Breakdown as of 11 June 1999, ASIS.

across a broad spectrum of organizations. This differs somewhat from women in public law enforcement, who tend to be in more stereotypical units such as sex crimes, juveniles, communications, and community related services. Of the women completing the ASIS membership information 7% indicated that they were currently in a public law enforcement or military position; 44% were in security and loss prevention positions; 34% identified themselves as in either executive/financial or other management positions; and the remaining 15% were represented in a variety of special areas such as sales, purchasing, and consultants.

The educational attainment for these ASIS women members is indicative of the notion that women tend to have more education than their male counterparts (Figure 4.3).

Private security may be seen as "employment that is privately funded, usually beginning where governmental or public security leaves off" (De Lucia and Doyle, 1998: 99). It has been described as one of the fastest growing professional careers worldwide, and as an industry it generates more than $100 billion a year.

Generally, private security is seen as more pro-active than public law enforcement, focusing efforts on prevention and environmental management to deter criminal activity (De Lucia and

Table 4.1   Company type—breakdown as of 11 June 1999, ASIS.

Type of Organization	Total Women Security Professionals
Architectural/Engineering Firm	7
Communication Services	123
Distribution/Warehousing	40
Educational Institution	85
Entertainment/Sports Facility	22
Financial Institution	127
Government/Administration	79
Law Enforcement	96
Government/Military	127
Health Care Facility	75
Hotel/Motel/Resort	42
Industrial/Manufacturing	224
Insurance	35
Oil/Gas/Mining Extraction	26
Real Estate	13
Research and Development	76
Security Service Guard and Technology	405
Security Consulting Firm	127
Transportation	24
Utilities	48

Doyle). Public law enforcement, on the other hand, has traditionally been seen as primarily reactive to crime, with less emphasis on prevention.

Hess and Wrobleski (1992) identify four major areas in which employment opportunities in private security exist: (1) retail security, (2) commercial security, (3) industrial security, and (4) institutional security. Four elements within each of these areas include: (1) physical security, (2) information security, (3) personnel security, and (4) information systems. Within each of these identified areas, there are four distinct skill sets or core competencies that every

Educational Attainment

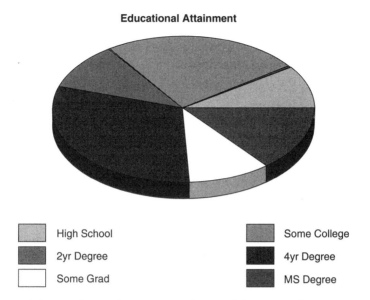

	High School		Some College
	2yr Degree		4yr Degree
	Some Grad		MS Degree

Figure 4.3. Highest Education Level—Breakdown as of 11 June 1999, ASIS.

security professional should possess: (1) management skills, (2) investigative skills, (3) technical security skills, and (4) protective skills.

Private security can also be either proprietary or contractual. The proprietary security professional is an employee of the company he or she is working for, and his or her salary and other benefits are paid by the organization. Contract security refers to companies that specialize in providing security officers and services to a corporation. In this case, security professionals are physically located at a particular organization but their salary and benefits are paid for by the contract security company. For example, the Microsoft Corporation may contract with Pinkerton Security to provide coverage of their facility 24 hours a day, seven days a week, 365 days per year. Pinkerton would hire the security staff, including the supervisors and managers necessary to adequately provide security for that site. The Pinkerton employees would generally work at Microsoft on a permanent basis, but would be paid by Pinkerton. They would not have the same benefits as the employees of Microsoft, but would be responsible for protecting Microsoft's physical and personal assets.

RETAIL SECURITY

Retail security managers, sometimes referred to as loss prevention managers or specialists, may be responsible for loss prevention within a single store or a chain of stores. Their job responsibilities include planning, training, and implementing numerous security tasks such as investigations of employee theft, customer shoplifting, and the placement and use of physical security technology, such as closed circuit television (CCTV) (Collins, Ricks, and Van Meter, 2000).

Employment opportunities in retail are numerous due to the magnitude of losses, which are estimated in excess of $30 billion per year. Opportunities for employment in retail can be with the store itself or with contract security companies offering "shopping services." A shopping service is used to detect internal theft by having an employee of the shopping service pose as a customer and creating situations for cashiers that test their honesty. For example, a "shopper" might act as though he or she is in a hurry and quickly go through a checkout, putting down the exact amount for an item in cash and declining a receipt. The cashier is then given an opportunity either to record the transaction and put the money into the cash register or, if he or she is dishonest, simply to put the money into his or her pocket.

There are a variety of job opportunities in retail security, ranging from the uniformed security officer, to the undercover or store detective, to the store or regional loss prevention manager. These positions consist of minimizing losses due to both internal and external theft, risk and physical security assessments, interviewing and interrogation skills, audits, and detection of shoplifters.

According to the American Society for Industrial Security Web-Pages a "Typical Retail Security Professional" has the following:

Education	Four-year degree
Experience	10–15 years
Specialty Experience	8–10 years
Professional Certification	Certified Protection Professional
Salary	$35,000–$60,000
Titles	Manager Protection, Director of Security, District Manager, Vice President of Security, Facility Security Manager, Loss Prevention Supervisor, or Loss Control Manager

COMMERCIAL SECURITY

Commercial security includes financial institutions, office buildings, hotels, recreational parks, transportation systems, airports, and airlines. Each of these institutions has unique security requirements.

Financial Institutions

Financial institutions are regulated by the Bank Protection Act of 1968, which calls for very specific security requirements. Banking security professionals are required to investigate both internal and external incidents of theft involving recovery of "bad" checks, credit card fraud, property recovery, and cases of employee embezzlement. Financial fraud and embezzlement are estimated at nearly $200 billion annually. According to the ASIS Professional Development: Security Specialty Areas WebPages the "Typical Financial Services Security Professional" has the following:

Education	Bachelor's, often a Master's, Degree
Experience	10 years
Specialty Experience	5–10 years
Professional Certification	Certified Fraud Examiner (CFE)
Salary Range	$35,000–$100,000
Title	Manager, Assistant Manager, Vice President, Security Officer, Investigator, Director, or Assistant Director

Office Buildings

Office buildings include both governmental and nongovernmental buildings. Governmental buildings and holdings are seldom protected by public law enforcement personnel. Most governmental buildings rely on proprietary or a contract security agencies for all of their building security needs. The use of private security is commonplace even for some military installations. Security concerns for both public and private office buildings range from vandalism and theft to the threat of terrorism. One need only remember the tragic bombing of the Alfred P. Murrah Federal Building in Oklahoma City to understand the extent of the threat (Collins, Ricks, and Van Meter, 2000).

Office buildings, unlike other types of institutions, need a greater amount of control with regard to ingress and egress of tenants and patrons. In a federal building there are numerous governmental offices that range from the social security office to the office of the Secret Service. With the use of certain physical security systems such as access control devices, closed circuit television (CCTV), and intrusion detection systems, the movement of people and the control of property are made much easier. The major security problems for commercial office buildings are after-hours burglaries, thefts, and incidents of internal theft. Security professionals employed in this type of work environment are required to be well versed in physical security technology, access control procedures, risk assessment, and emergency preparedness planning.

Hotel Security

Hotel security, much like hospital security, has many common security elements such as retail, food service, parking security, and the protection of guests and their belongings. In some cases such as with resorts or casinos, they have additional issues such as the handling of large sums of money, a large open facility with numerous entryways, swimming pools, bars, theaters, conference rooms, and offices, all of which fall under the protection of the security staff.

The primary responsibility of the security department or staff is to provide their patrons with a safe and secure environment. Many of the problems facing hotels and resorts are similar to problems cited in other types of organizations: internal and external theft of property, vandalism of property, and parking garage thefts from guests' automobiles. Although the aforementioned represent the greatest threat, there is also the concern for guest safety from assault or injury.

Hotel security personnel must be well versed in risk assessment, investigation skills, access control systems (computer-generated key systems), security procedures, and policies for pre-employment screening, cleaning staff, handling of cash and/or valuables, fire and safety regulations, physical security systems (such as CCTV), safeguarding guest property, parking lot security, and oversight of other resort properties, such as casinos. Casinos represent one of the more complex types of hotel security because of their unique characteristics, such as being open 24 hours per day every day year round. These can be exceptionally large, such as the MGM Casino and Hotel in Las Vegas. The gaming/wagering security professional has the following demographics from the American Society for Industrial Security WebPages:

Education	Undergraduate Degree
Experience	10–15 years
Specialty Experience	6–8 years
Professional Certification	Gaming Commission License
Salary	$30,000–$60,000
Title	Director of Security, Security Officer, Loss Prevention Director, or Manager of Security

Recreational Parks

Recreational parks have matured from the traveling carnival to complex theme parks that could be classified as an entire city or community. The best example is Walt Disney World, which has locations worldwide. At the Orlando, Florida, complex alone there are over 46 square miles with three separate theme parks: the Magic Kingdom Park, Epcot, and the Disney-MGM Studios. There are also water parks, a shopping area, two nighttime entertainment complexes, and 16 different hotels. Clearly security for a facility as diverse and as complex as this requires a multifaceted security staff. Today, many of the larger amusement parks provide numerous opportunities for a person pursuing a career in amusement park security.

Transportation Systems

Transportation systems refer to the billions of tons of cargo that are processed by sea, land, and air in this country daily. One of the greatest concerns for transportation security professionals is the theft or loss of property. According to the FBI, cargo theft accounts for more than $14 billion in losses annually. "The indirect costs of claims processing, capital tied up in claims and litigation, and market losses from both non-delivery and underground competition from stolen goods are estimated at $93 billion annually" (Fisher and Green, 1998: 393). The majority of lost commodities falls into one of the following categories: clothing, camera and video equipment, tobacco, and alcoholic beverages. The breakdown of theft for each industry is as follows: 22% from clothing and textiles, 17% from food, and 10% from jewelry (Fisher and Green, 1998: 397).

Transportation security professionals must work closely with rail police, state and local police, customs, and other federal officials. Security professionals working in this area must be experienced in transportation accountability systems; Department of Transportation guidelines; background screening of drivers and other employees; policies and procedures for the prevention of theft and pilferage; physical security technology systems for transportation; access control to docks and terminal areas; risk assessments and security surveys; policies and procedures while in transit; and proper use of seals and locks for trucks, containers, and air cargo containers.

Airports and airlines were some of the first types of commercial properties to advocate the use of security in the 1960s. During this time, skyjacking became a serious threat to disrupting airline operations in this country. By the late 1960s, skyjacking had reached an all-time high in the United States, with the majority of the skyjacked flights being forced to land in Cuba. One of the most famous cases of skyjacking was perpetrated in November of 1971 when Dan Cooper hijacked a plane after boarding in Portland, Oregon, for a flight to Seattle, Washington. The case still remains open after Cooper, donning a parachute and a bag full of money, jumped from the airliner over the mountainous terrain between Seattle, Washington, and Reno, Nevada.

The federal response to this incident and the others that preceded it was to pass the Anti-Hijacking Act of 1974 and the Air Transportation Security Act of 1974, which permitted the President of the United States to suspend summarily, without notice or hearing, for an indeterminate period of time, the right of any carrier to engage in air transportation between the United States and any nation that permits its lands to be used by terrorist organizations or that promotes or engages in air piracy. In 1975, additional legislation, FAR 129 (Foreign Air Corridor Security Program), was passed, which mandated that all foreign air carriers landing in and departing from the United States screen all passengers and carry-on luggage.

Most airline security professionals work for the airline carriers, who are responsible for providing security. The carrier must secure not only the airplane but the concourse as well. A 1990 amendment to the Federal Aviation Act of 1958 requires airport operators and carriers to have a security program that incorporates the following security procedures: a written and approved plan for the safety of persons and property traveling in air transportation and intrastate air transportation against acts of criminal violence and aircraft piracy; that the program includes a description of the procedures, facilities, and equipment used to perform the security control functions required of the airport operator and of each air carrier having security responsibility over an exclusive area; and that it includes a description of emergency and contingency plans, law enforcement support necessary, and the training that law enforcement is to receive to be in compliance with regulations.

The bombing of Pan Am Flight 103 in 1988 over Lockerbie, Scotland, painfully reminded Americans that we are still vulnerable to the long arm of terrorism. This tragic incident resulted in the death of 192 and the injury of 40 more and did more to heighten security awareness among the airline industry and to help tighten airline security in this country.

INDUSTRIAL SECURITY

Industrial security often refers to large organizations such as General Motors or General Electric that employ proprietary security forces. However, in the last decade many of the Fortune 500 companies have made a move to downsize their proprietary security staff and augment it with more sophisticated physical security systems and contract security companies. These types of organizations tend to depend on a small but professional security staff. Positions often require advanced degrees and 5 to 10 years of applicable experience. An industrial security professional must be well versed in specific industrial standards and guidelines and have a multidisciplinary knowledge of safety management and regulations. In addition to development of policies and procedures for the protection of company assets, the security professional must be well equipped to address internal theft of equipment, products, and confidential information such as trade secrets or government classified information. The security manager and staff play a critical role in conducting background or pre-employment screening of personnel. Some industrial environments such as utility and transportation require the security staff to design and make operational complex security systems that attempt to reduce loss, monitor access, and control and deter crime.

The new challenge facing security professionals in industry and many other types of organizations is the protection of information, especially with regard to the Internet and global access. This has resulted in an entirely new field within not only the industrial setting but many others as well: computer security. This is an entire profession in and of itself. Many corporations are recruiting people to develop a secure operating environment and make decisions with regard to the design or purchase of secure operating systems. This has become imperative with the movement toward electronic commerce and trade. The nation's increased reliance on computers has made security networks, financial institutions, and power grids more vulnerable to computer attacks.

Within industrial security is a professional discipline referred to as Government Industrial Security, which involves the classification, declassification, and protection of national security information that is in the possession of government classified contractors. These are companies that are contracted by federal government agencies such as the Department of Defense or the Department of Energy to design, develop, manufacture, or test government classified equipment or systems. Government industrial security professionals protect special categories of classified information, including restricted data, formerly restricted data, intelligence sources and methods information, sensitive compartmented information, and special access program information (ASIS Online: Professional Development WebPages).

Typically the industrial security and government industrial security professional has the following demographics:

Education	Undergraduate Degree
Experience	5–10 years
Specialty Experience	5–10 years
Professional Certification	Completed DOD and DOE Courses
Salary Range	$35,000–$70,000+
Titles	Security Manager, Director of Security, Security Force Supervisor, Plant Protection Manager, Investigator, Security Specialist, Facilities Security Officer, or Industrial Security Specialist

INSTITUTIONAL SECURITY

Organizations that are open to the public have unique security concerns. An example is health care facilities, which are estimated at well over 30,000 in the United States. These include both public and privately owned hospitals, clinics, nursing homes, outpatient centers, and physicians' office complexes. Health care is considered to be the fifth largest industry in this country.

The hospital security professional is focused on patient protection and services that include maintaining accountability and inventory control of both hospital and patient property; providing for the protection of such areas as emergency rooms, newborn nurseries, pharmacies, and controlled substances storage; areas containing radioactive materials; and the hospital mortuary.

Hospital security professionals must also be in compliance with the Joint Commission on Accreditation of Healthcare Organizations (JCAHO). This agency serves as the primary accrediting organization for hospitals. The hospital security professional must be knowledgeable of the reporting requirements set forth by JCAHO. Specific security and safety standards are required for what JCAHO refers to as the "environment of care" and include the elements that must be addressed in a written security management program:

+ Description of security concerns regarding patients, visitors, personnel, and property.
+ A system for identification of patients, visitors, and staff.
+ Access control and physical security for sensitive areas such as the emergency room, newborn nursery, etc.
+ Provide vehicular and traffic control to the emergency service area.
+ Designate personnel who are responsible for the development, implementation, and monitoring of the security plan.
+ Describe the procedure for reporting and investigating all security incidents.
+ Provide for the annual evaluation of the hospital security plan.

In addition to the Joint Commission Environment of Care Plans for security and safety inspections, the hospital security professional must provide training to all hospital staff on issues such as workplace violence, emergency preparedness, life safety management, and potential bomb threats, especially with regard to abortion clinics or research and testing facilities in which animals are used.

The "Typical Healthcare Security Professional" demographics from ASIS Online Professional Development WebPages are:

Education	Undergraduate Degree
Experience	12–15 years
Specialty Experience	8–10 years
Professional Certification	Certified Health Professional
Salary Range	$50,000–$75,000
Titles	Director of Hospital Security, Director of Security, Security Chief, Security Manager, Director of Safety and Security, Director of HR/Security, and Security Services Manager

SECURITY SALARIES

Although data is not available for salaries of security professionals based on gender, the industry standard is that security directors or managers with policymaking authority normally make only about $70,000 per year. The average 1996 security executive has 25 or more years of experience and a graduate degree (M.S. or Ph.D.), and has a professional certification such as Certified Protection Professional (CPP) or Certified Fraud Examiner (CFE). There are numerous cases, however, where security directors make over $250,000 per year (Langer, 1996: 76). The chart in Figure 4.4 details the average annual income of security directors by (1) size of organization, and (2) level of education.

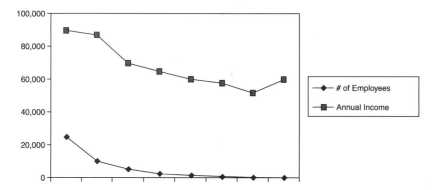

Figure 4.4. Average annual income of security director by size of organization. (Adapted from the August 1996 issue of *Security Management,* American Society for Industrial Security, 1655 North Fort Myer Drive, Suite 1200, Arlington, VA 22209).

Women considering employment and promotion in the security profession should possess the aforementioned skill sets or core competencies: (1) management and leadership skills, (2) investigative skills, (3) technical security skills, and (4) protective skills. Although these cannot guarantee success or promotion, they represent the professional skills necessary to gain entry into the profession. Women should also plan on obtaining an undergraduate degree in a security-related professional program such as security management, computer and information security, criminal justice, business, law, computer science, or a technical degree.

5

Research

Research on women in law enforcement is limited, with the primary focus being on women in large municipal police departments and with little emphasis on state or federal law enforcement. Empirical data examining women in private security is all but nonexistent. The existing research has examined issues of competency, attitudes toward and of women in policing, stress, legal issues, or simply provided descriptions of the current population of women officers or guards. This research has taken the form of survey research, evaluation research, participant observation, and qualitative case studies. In addition to the paucity of research, Morash and Greene (1986) have assessed the validity of previous work and identified gender bias in some of these works. The following chapter identifies and summarizes previous research on women in law enforcement, with a larger focus on women in public municipal policing. Because there is such limited work on women in private security, a comparison is made of women in private security to women in corrections, as the two professions can be described as analogous.

WOMEN IN PUBLIC LAW ENFORCEMENT

Competency and Attitudes Toward Women Officers

When women entered patrol, their performance was questioned because their gender role was not consistent with the definition of policing as a masculine occupation. It is at this point that the impetus to evaluate women in policing began. By focusing primarily on the issue of competency, this research attempted to determine whether women were capable of performing the job. Morash and Green (1986) identified nine evaluations of women's performance that were designed to assess whether women could effectively perform as uniformed patrol officers on the street in various jurisdictions. The jurisdictions included Washington, D.C. (Bloch and Anderson, 1974), St. Louis (Sherman, 1975), New York City (Sichel, Friedman, Quint, and Smith, 1977), Denver (Bartlett and Rosenblum, 1977), Newton, Massachusetts (Kizziah and Morris, 1977), Philadelphia—Phase I and Phase II (Bartell Associates, 1978), California (California Highway Patrol, 1976), and Pennsylvania (Pennsylvania State Police, 1974). All of these studies found that females perform as effectively as males, with one exception: Philadelphia, Phase II. This particular study was the second phase of the Pennsylvania study (Morash and Green, 1986).

Bloch and Anderson (1974) conducted the first study pertaining to the competency of women in policing. They examined effectiveness in terms of the most important job of all police roles: the job of patrol (p. i). Their study compared the performance of 86 female and 86 male police officers in the Washington, D.C., metropolitan police department. The study used several measures of performance to evaluate a range of tasks, including arrest rates, levels of patrol activity, and driving ability. They also examined personnel records to assess performance evaluations. In addition, observers rode with police officers in a variety of situations ranging from public relations to violent activities. Finally, they asked supervisors about their perceptions of the women officers' competency. The study concluded that women and men performed their jobs quite similarly and that women were as competent as their male counterparts.

Several researchers have performed similar studies (Ayoob, 1978; Bartlett and Rosenblum, 1977; California Highway Patrol, 1976; Hickman, 1978; Rutland, 1978; Sherman, 1975). All of these studies have compared male and female police officers and evaluated their performance using a variety of indicators. These indicators have included patrol observations and departmental records, as well as perceptions of the public and other police officers. All of these studies conclude that female police officers are as competent as male police officers; they indicate that female police officers perform the job effectively.

Using objective criteria, female police officers are judged to be competent. However, some research suggests that male police officers believe that females are ineffective and incompetent. Bloch and Anderson (1974), for example, report that male officers feel that they can handle violent situations better than females and that male officers preferred not to work with female officers. It appears that some male officers question the competency of female officers because they believe that females cannot physically handle the job due to their relative lack of physical strength. Balkin (1988) reports that police officers have negative attitudes toward female police officers and that these attitudes reflect concerns about female officers' lack of physical strength. Further studies (Hindman, 1975; Linden, 1984; Vega and Silverman, 1982) have found that some male officers also believe that female police officers are not aggressive enough for police work. Martin (1980) found that most male police officers are traditionals who emphasize the law enforcement aspect of the job and have more stereotypical views of women; these men oppose women in policing because they believe that female officers are physically weak, unreliable, unaggressive, and generate fewer arrests. Furthermore, differences in size and strength appear to influence opinions regarding women's competency in dangerous situations (Charles and Parsons, 1978).

The public has also responded with negative reactions, saying that since women are physically weaker, they will be unable to handle dangerous situations (Bell, 1982: 215). The public generally believes, however, that female police officers can have a calming effect in adverse circumstances (Bell, 1982).

Snortum and Beyers (1983) found no difference between male and female officers on traffic stops, pedestrian checks, vehicle stops, or other patrolling observations. They found only two differences between women and men. The first was that during the first tour of duty men were dispatched to more high risk calls than were women, but this difference appeared for officers who worked for longer periods, thus, gaining more experience. The other difference occurred in the second and third tours of duty for those working at the station. To see if women were being diverted to sex-role stereotyped activities, Snortum and Beyers examined categories of activities and looked for patterns of over- and underutilization. Women were found to be overutilized in a few activities: in prisoner searches and in crimes dealing with women and children, such as rape and child abuse. Overutilization for prisoner searches was deemed acceptable by the researchers and was attributed to the fact that there were no female jailers to search female prisoners, so women had to be called to assist. Snortum and Beyers (1983) concluded that the overutilization in other categories was also appropriate. They found as well that there were no activities in which women were under-utilized or any significant differences in any major areas of self-initiated patrol activities: traffic stops, pedestrian checks, vehicle stops, and other observations (Snortum and Beyers, 1983).

In contemporary research that examines attitudes toward women in policing more broadly, Haarr (1997) used qualitative research methods, consisting of field observations and in-depth interviews, to examine the effects of race and gender on patterns of inter-personal interaction in a police patrol bureau, and the factors that affect the integration of women and blacks into the bureau. In a medium-sized Midwest police department, she interviewed and observed 47 patrol officers, both women and men, and blacks and whites. Interviews and observations consisted of items to obtain and assess demographic information, the police patrol culture, and patterns of interaction.

Haarr (1997) found that white male officers interact most frequently with other white male officers. Black males tended to interact more with males generally and black males in particular. Black females interacted most with other black females and black males, with limited interaction with white males. White females interacted with other white females and white males most often. Both white and black females tended to socialize less during work hours than males. A majority of the officers recognized gender and race divisions in the department.

When trying to identify explanations for the lack of integration in the police organization, Haarr (1997) found that officers attributed this lack to: (1) affirmative action and dual promotion lists, (2) the decision-making process for job assignments, (3) lack of maternity leave policy for women, (4) conflict between the Police Officers Association and the Afro-American Police League, and (5) sexism and the marginalization of women in patrol (Haarr, 1997: 67). Both white males and females agreed that there was discrimination in the promotion process and had resentment toward black officers. Their reason for resentment was that black officers were promoted through affirmative action and not for merit. White male officers claimed to suffer adverse effects in job assignments more than women or blacks. Male respondents, in fact, attributed some job assignments to some females' use of their sexuality and simply their gender in explaining why women receive certain opportunities or assignments. Some women expressed dissatisfaction with regard to the lack of or inadequate pregnancy leave policy.

Regarding the police organizations, every officer was required to be a member of the police union, while black officers could also be members of the Afro-American Police League, which served as a support league for its members. The black league often addressed issues that it felt the union did not address adequately, and some white officers felt that the black league threatened the police union. These dynamics provided the basis for much of the segregated interaction in the police organization (Haarr, 1997).

Both black and white males expressed negative attitudes toward women on patrol, especially with respect to women's abilities to handle the physical demands of the job and to provide safety under all circumstances. Women in the department were well aware of these attitudes, and unfortunately were marginalized because of them;

sexual harassment was one of the most frequent ways women officers were marginalized. From the research, Haarr (1997: 79) concludes that "No single structural, political, or individual characteristic or condition appears to be a decisive cause for women's and blacks' lack of integration into the patrol bureau," and that officers are "divided by race and gender differences, coupled with features of organizational life such as tension, conflict, and intraorganizational feuding over affirmative action, dual promotion lists, the decision-making process related to job assignments, police leagues in the department, and the presence of women on patrol" (p. 79).

Additional research examining the competency of women used supervisor evaluations in small town police departments, which also rated a sample of 30 women and 30 men as having equal performance on eleven measures (Bartol, Bergen, Volckens, and Knoras, 1992). Other differences between women and men include observations that women were more communicative, less violent, and more respectful toward citizens (Belknap and Shelley, 1993). Some research indicates that male officers received more citizen complaints (Bartlett and Rosenblum, 1977), were more willing to use their guns, met more resistance than female officers (Felkenes and Schroeder, 1993; for a review, see Lunnenborg, 1989; Morash and Greene, 1986), and have higher arrest rates than women (Bloch and Anderson, 1974; Sherman, 1975).

Ott (1989) studied tokenism in Dutch policing and nursing. This work tested Kanter's (1977) theory of numerical imbalance and the concept of critical mass to assess whether or not these are gender-neutral. She examined two professions that were considered gender appropriate for both sexes, policing and nursing, so that sufficient numbers of both sexes, skewed (minority is less than 15%) and tilted (minority represents 15–35%) groups, could be tested. The effects of critical mass could also be tested by comparing these groups in the same types of settings. Variables under consideration included: resistance, visibility, informal contacts, stress, and sex-role stereotyping.

Ott (1989) interviewed 150 police women and men (50 groups of three) who worked in 15 member patrol teams, and 147 nurses

(49 teams of three). With respect to the police teams, three people from each team were interviewed; each group was comprised of one woman, one man, and the sergeants (all of whom were men but one). The teams were divided into two groups: O groups and F groups. O teams had only one woman on the team, while F teams had a few women on the team. Teams averaged no more than four women per team. Ott (1989) hypothesized that O women officers would experience disadvantages, and that F men would oppose increases in the number of women more than O male officers, because the numbers of women were moving away from token status and moving closer to the critical mass.

Two areas in which O and F women did not differ were in stress and absenteeism. In other areas there were differences in the O and F women. O women felt more visible, paid more attention to their male colleagues, and had fewer informal contacts than F women. O women more often doubted their competency and whether a male and female team could handle all calls than did F women. O women indicated that they felt less accepted, were subject to more sexual harassment, and had problems with gossip more often than F women.

Most F men wanted to keep the number of women in the organization as it was and preferred that a man be hired before a woman. On the other hand, O men wanted more women in the organization and had no preference with regards to hiring a woman or man. Ott (1989) indicates that women were supportive of each other, whether there were two, three, or four of them on a team, without any evidence of rivalry.

The results of Ott's (1989) work contradict Kanter's hypothesis that the theory of numerical imbalance and the concept of critical mass apply to both men and women in minority positions and are therefore gender-neutral. Regarding the dynamics of proportion, however, Kanter's work was supported. Specifically, the smaller the number of individuals in the minority group, the greater the differences between the minority and majority appear to be. However, Kanter (1977) claimed that the dynamics of proportion always affected the minority group negatively. Ott (1989), on the other hand, found this was not the case for men in the minority. She contends that the differences she encountered are effects of the high correlation between gender and status, the stereotypes that exist about the majority and minority, the kind of work that is being done and the way the work is structured.

Wertsch (1998) also examined tokenism as a barrier to advancement in policing through interviews with women in a medium-sized Pacific Northwest city. This work was an exploratory study of 16 women in the police organization that was intended to guide future research of tokenism in the workplace. Wertsch found that tokenism may act as one of several confounding factors that contribute to women's advancement in policing. Specifically, tokenism as a barrier may have a detrimental effect under the following conditions: when (1) the organization's promotional mechanisms are unequal and discriminatory; (2) the organization's promotional mechanisms are equal and nondiscriminatory and allow for the advancement of women, but the effects of tokenism are enough to deter individuals from competing for advancement; and (3) competition for advancement is perceived as equal, but the combination of tokenism and formal policies tends to direct women towards a specific unit (Wertsch, 1998: 53–54).

Respondents indicated that certain elements of a token's role, such as role entrapment, stereotyping, isolation, and performance pressures, affected the amount of stress, frustration, and dissatisfaction that are frequently experienced by women in policing. To examine role entrapment and stereotyping, Wertsch (1998) asked respondents to describe calls that they were typically assigned by a dispatcher. The majority of the women indicated that domestic violence incidents, sexual assault reports, and traffic accident/reports were their main service calls. Furthermore, the women perceived male officers as more likely to be assigned calls such as assaults in progress that were nonsexual and perpetrators with gun. Respondents indicated that they perceived dispatchers as making assignments based on stereotypical assumptions regarding the female officers' capabilities (Wertsch, 1998). Further examination revealed that the respondents perceived that taking positions such as Drug

Abuse Resistance Education (D.A.R.E) officers or Neighborhood Resource Officers (N.R.O.), which are stereotypically perceived as appropriate for female assignments, often contributed to a decrease in their credibility since these units do not provide opportunities for real police work.

A majority of respondents in Wertsch's (1998) study indicated that they were not accepted by their male counterparts, which resulted in isolation. Both covert behavior, such as gossiping, and overt behavior, such as being left out of group activities, were identified by the women as contributing to isolation. Regarding performance pressure, a majority of those interviewed felt that they had to work harder than their male counterparts, while slightly over half of the respondents indicated that they felt more visible than their male counterparts, thus requiring them to work harder than the males. Finally, all respondents in this research indicated that they were obligated to prove themselves to dubious male officers upon entering police work (Wertsch, 1998: 40).

Wertsch (1998) concluded that an officer's token status may be a contributory factor creating structural barriers for advancement and that advancement may be adversely affected by the conditions previously stated regarding the organization's promotional mechanisms and employees' perception of advancement.

Scarborough and Hemmens (1998) examined gender differences in Section 1983 claims, federal civil rights claims, against law enforcement officers in the United States Circuit Courts of Appeals from 1989–1993. Data consisted of cases involving woman officers as sole defendants. The following variables were described by gender: types of issues most frequently litigated; whether decisions were based on procedural or substantive decisions; types of agencies most frequently sued; issues that resulted in the most successful outcomes against law enforcement; the amount and types of damages awarded; and the circuit in which the case originated.

Women constituted only 8% of the defendants in these cases, and some of the cases had both male and female defendants. Six cases had only female defendants, representing only 1% of the population. The most frequently litigated issue against these women, constituting 24% of the issues, were claims of unlawful search and seizure, followed closely by claims of excessive force (22%), and false arrest claims (19%). These three issues represented 65% of the claims against women; eleven other issues constituted the remaining 35%, but none represented more than 5% of the total claims. Seventy-five percent of the issues were decided based on substantive issues, while the remaining were based on procedure. Women officers came from municipal agencies in 65% of the cases, 24% worked for sheriff's departments, while the remaining 11% worked for other types of agencies such as federal or state. Police officers or agencies prevailed in 55% of the cases against them. Twenty-three percent of the time the cases were remanded to the federal district courts for further consideration. Awards were identified for only 11% of the incidents and ranged from nominal awards of $1 to $860,500 for damages. Four of the circuits had over 10% of the cases in their respective regions. Almost one-fifth of the cases originated in the Ninth Circuit, which includes: Alaska, Arizona, California, Hawaii, Idaho, Montana, Nevada, Oregon, and Washington. The Tenth Circuit, which includes Colorado, Kansas, New Mexico, Oklahoma, Utah, and Wyoming, contained 17% of the incidents. The Eighth and Second Circuits both originated 11% of the cases.

When comparing the numbers of women and men in these suits to their proportion in the population, it appears that both were proportionately represented. Although the gender of plaintiffs and defendants has not been the focus of civil liability in law enforcement, these findings do appear to contradict related research where women have been found to have fewer citizen complaints than men. In addition, the Christopher Commission in their examination of the Los Angeles Police Department found that women were underrepresented in complaints of excessive force. It is possible that citizen complaints are an inadequate proxy measure for litigation. Individuals are not required to file a complaint through the police department prior to litigation, and no prior research has examined the correlation between citizen complaints and litigation.

Perhaps plaintiffs are more prone to litigate cases involving women because the women are acting contradictory to stereotypical perceptions, which portray them as demure, weak individuals, unlike the powerful, masculine type that has traditionally been associated with the police role (Martin, 1980). Female officers may be acting within the confines of legal behavior but behaving outside of the range of what is acceptably female. Thus these women are perceived as violating the law, when in fact they are doing nothing more than violating societal expectations. Additionally, women in nontraditional occupations such as policing are often the subject of negative attitudes and/or sexual harassment by their male counterparts for numerous reasons. If negative attitudes of fellow male officers are perceived by possible litigants, this may encourage the litigants to pursue complaints against women. Also, in cases involving both female and male officers, potential litigants (especially those who are also suspects or arrestees), may try to gain favor by adversely reacting to female officers as a show of support for male officers. Consequently, if citizens also accept that in circumstances where both male and female officers are present, the male officer will be the one with the most power, it would be logical that they would be less antagonistic toward male officers, in hopes of improving their position in the eyes of the male officer. Given the contradictory nature of the findings, further research should be conducted to better understand the gendered nature of civil litigation.

Similarly, Lersch (1998) examined complaints of misconduct filed against police officers in a large Southeast department to assess the existence and extent of differences in female and male officers. Using citizen allegations of misconduct filed against officers with an internal affairs unit, the following areas were examined: gender distribution of complaints, differences in age, race, or tenure in officers named in allegations, differences in complaint characteristics, and differences in characteristics of citizens filing complaints of misconduct.

Lersch (1998) evaluated a total of 527 complaints, which, because more than one officer may have been involved in the complaint, translated into 682 allegations of misconduct. The period of analysis was three years, from 1992 to 1994. The complaints were categorized into four categories: (1) those involving force; (2) nonviolent complaints involving threatening behavior, harassment, and discourtesy; (3) dereliction in the performance of duties; and (4) miscellaneous complaints that ranged in allegations from inappropriate driving to conducting personal affairs while on duty. The department consisted of a majority of male officers (87.6%).

Regarding the gender distribution of the alleged complaints, Lersch (1998) found that male officers were overrepresented in the alleged complaints. Only 5.7% of the alleged complaints were against female officers, which is almost 7% less representation than in the entire law policing population. No significant gender differences were found with respect to age or tenure. Significant differences were found, however, for race, with minority males being overrepresented. Neither complaint type nor type of initiation was a significant predictor of gender in this research. Lersch, however, did find that women were more likely to receive a citizen's complaint following a proactive encounter with a citizen. These findings are similar to those of Scarborough and Hemmens (1998), as discussed earlier. Citizen race or gender was not a significant predictor of officer gender.

Additional attitudinal research conducted by Leger (1997) examined citizens' perceptions of women in policing in two Kentucky counties. She used a 17-question telephone survey to assess attitudes of a random sample of respondents generated from the telephone book. Leger (1997) obtained 200 responses from 600 calls. She asked respondents their views on the dangers of police work; the appropriateness of police work as an occupation for women; and the physical ability, competency, respect for citizens, and sympathy for crime victims of women police officers. Leger reported a general overall positive attitude toward women in policing with an apparent decrease in skeptical attitudes toward women's abilities to handle violent encounters, when compared to previous research.

Specifically, Leger (1997) found that the majority of respondents felt that police work is an appropriate occupation for women and that women are able to effectively handle violent encounters.

Respondents also strongly support the promotion of qualified female officers and an increase or at least maintenance of the number of women on patrol. A majority of respondents did not agree with the statement that female police officers do not have the physical ability to be effective on patrol (Leger, 1997: 242). Respondents overwhelmingly agree that female police officers are able to make competent decisions in emergency situations and that female officers are more respectful to citizens than their male counterparts. A majority of respondents also indicated that they felt safe with female officers on patrol. Although Leger indicates that a majority of the respondents had never been assisted or apprehended by a female police officer, she concludes that the attitudes in this study are likely to be a product of a more general view of women (Leger, 1997: 244).

Attitudes Toward Police Work

Research comparing the attitudes of women and men in police work is more limited than evaluation research examining the competency of women on patrol or attitudes toward women in policing. Attitudinal research has not consistently supported or negated differences in women and men (Bloch and Anderson, 1974; Worden, 1993). Worden (1993) found few differences in officers' perceptions of the public, their occupational roles, coworkers, and police organizations (Martin and Jurik, 1996). Women and men were both disfavorable toward restrictions on their independence and discretion, and both had positive attitudes toward the public. Differences in women's and men's attitudes include women having lower expectations of promotion and lacking self-confidence in handling a variety of police incidents (Worden, 1993).

In Worden's (1993) examination of police officer attitudes using data from the 1977 Police Services Study, she evaluated the following attitudes: perceptions of the police role, perceptions of citizens, evaluations of coworkers and departments, and occupational integration. Worden contends that proposed differences in female and male attitudes have not been empirically supported. In other words, those who assert that women bring a different set of values and attitudes to the job are basing their hypothesis more on assumption than empirical evidence. The results of this work indicate that there are few differences in women's and men's attitudes toward their role, the public, or their departments. Furthermore, women and men are not equally integrated into their jobs. With regard to the police role, there were no significant differences by gender when examining the acceptance of legal restrictions and broad role orientation. Differences were moderately significant in three variables measuring acceptance of rules and authority, uniform enforcement (versus selective enforcement), and noneconomic incentive. Women officers were more likely to believe that police officers perform better when they have clear rules and orders to follow, and they tend to favor uniform enforcement of the law (Worden, 1993: 219). There were no significant differences between women and men regarding their attitudes toward the public or their coworkers. When examining attitudes toward their workplace, Worden found that women were more likely to have a more positive attitude toward their workplace than men did (statistically significant). This finding suggests that if women's perceptions of their jobs are negatively affected by the difficulties they encounter, they are nonetheless less critical (Worden, 1993: 224).

Although Worden (1993) recognizes the possible limitations of this work, noting that attitudes of women and men in law enforcement may have changed somewhat since 1977, she contends that, "taken as a whole, these findings offer little support for the thesis that female officers define their role, or see their clientele, differently than males do, and one must therefore remain skeptical (albeit not disbelieving) about claims that women bring to their beats a distinctive perspective on policing" (Worden, 1993: 229).

Zhao, Thurman, and He (1999) examined job satisfaction in a medium-sized police department in the Northeast. They found no significant differences by gender or race with respect to satisfaction with work, satisfaction with supervisors, or satisfaction with coworkers. Other studies found that women and minority officers are less satisfied with their jobs than others (Buzawa, 1984; Buzawa,

Austin, and Bannon, 1994), while Belknap and Shelley (1992) report that an officer's job satisfaction may be related to the number of women in the organization.

In a survey of members of the International Association of Women Police, Grant, Garrison, and McCormick (1990) examined perceptions of utilization and job satisfaction. They found a significant and high correlation between utilization and job satisfaction. Job satisfaction was also significantly correlated with rank, opportunities for special assignments and training, number of different assignments held, and number of tactical units to which officers were assigned, although these correlations were lower than that of utilization. Rank had the lowest correlation with job satisfaction, and the authors suggest that monetary rewards and recognition through advancement do not mean as much to women as do other factors, such as opportunities for and types of assignment. Recognizing that actual utilization of officers could not be compared due to the variety of organizations, Grant et al. (1990) contend that it is important to further examine *perceived* utilization of women officers. Although oftentimes external factors such as total manpower and budget constraints can limit utilization, it is likely that "a better understanding of the operation of the department as a whole would change perceptions of utilization," and possibly practices as well (Grant et al., 1990: 150).

In a 1997 study, Dantzker and Kubin (1998) examined job satisfaction by gender from data collected from a national sample of municipal police officers. The data included responses from 2,734 police officers in seven states representing 14 municipalities. The organizations ranged in size from 30 to 1,500. Among the respondents, 87.4% were men and 11.3% were women.

Dantzker and Kubin (1998) found that women were less satisfied with their jobs, but the difference was not statistically significant. In one area, extras (Insurance, Overtime, Compensation, Off-Duty Job Policy, and Educational Incentive), women were more satisfied, but the difference was not statistically significant. Men were more satisfied in three areas: General Administration (Retirement, Selection, Salary, Supervisors, etc.), Equipment (Quality and Availability of) and Job (Reporting, Assignment, General Job Description), with the difference in Equipment for women and men being statistically significant. Gender by itself was not significantly related to job satisfaction; however, when combined with other demographic variables, it was. For Job Satisfaction, gender was statistically significant when combined with rank, age, and years of experience. Regarding general administration, gender was statistically significant when combined with rank, age, years of experience, and education. Gender was statistically related to equipment when combined with rank and ethnicity and also to Job when combined with rank and years of experience. Dantzker and Kubin (1998) indicate, however, that the variables only accounted for 6% or less of the variance in each of the models, and that there may be other variables influencing job satisfaction. This research supports previous research (Worden, 1993) indicating that gender has little relationship to job satisfaction (Dantzker and Kubin, 1998).

Gossett and Williams (1998) explored female officers' perception of discrimination in the police organization. Using snowball sampling, a technique used to identify potential respondents, they interviewed 27 female officers in a Southwestern metropolitan area. Six law enforcement agencies were represented, including metropolitan police departments, suburban departments, and sheriff's departments. The researchers addressed two primary questions: (1) Do female officers feel discriminated against, and if so, by whom? and (2) In what ways do female officers feel discriminated against (Gossett and Williams, 1998: 59)? Single interviews, lasting about 45 minutes, provided the data for this research. The researchers divided the sample into two groups based on whether or not the respondents indicated that they felt discriminated against. Seventeen of the officers indicated that they felt discriminated against, while 10 officers said they did not.

Of those officers who indicated that they felt discriminated against, the majority of them felt that their male coworkers, especially older, white officers, discriminated against them (Gossett and Williams, 1998: 63). Respondents also indicated that they felt discriminated against by citizens, administrators, and male supervisors.

Discrimination was characterized as being largely subtle and inadvertent, and significantly affected by the "good ol' boy" system (Gossett and Williams, 1998: 63). Many respondents indicated that older officers had told them that they should not be in law enforcement, and the women felt that male officers did not want women in positions of authority, which was demonstrated by a lack of recognition of authority. Most of the respondents indicated that they were quite frequently not taken seriously by their coworkers, and had had inappropriate behavior directed toward them. Regarding treatment by citizens, over half of the respondents who felt discriminated against indicated that citizens had requested a male officer when they responded to a call.

Of those officers who indicated that they had not experienced discrimination, one felt that discrimination depends on the agency, while some said that discrimination is an easy excuse (Gossett and Williams, 1998: 62). One respondent felt that women who complain about discrimination were crybabies (Gossett and Williams, 1998: 62). There was consensus among the respondents, however, that discrimination has changed over time, that it was not in the same form as it had been previously, and that it is more subtle and covert today.

Stress, Coping, and Police Work

Some research examining stress and police work has found that both levels of stress and primary stressors of women and men are similar (Morash and Haarr, 1995; Wexler and Logan, 1983; White and Marino, 1983). In contrast, other research indicates differences in stress levels of women and men (Pendergrass and Ostrove, 1984; Silbert, 1982).

In their study of stress among female police officers, Wexler and Logan (1983) interviewed 25 female police officers over a nine-month period in a large metropolitan department in California. The sources of stress among those women were categorized into four groups: external, organizational, task-related, and personal stressors. A fifth category was also added: female-related stressors, which are specific to female officers.

Organizational and female-related stressors were most often cited by these women as causing stress. Problems with training such as verbal abuse and intimidation were the most frequently mentioned organizational stressors. Negative attitudes of male officers, displayed by blatant ignoring of female officers, for example, were the most frequently cited female stressors. Rumors about female police officers, exposure to tragedy, and trouble associated with the job were also mentioned by over half the sample as a source of stress. Finally, group blame was a major source of stress for the female officers. These women often experience the stress of minority group status. When one female officer made a mistake, all female officers suffered. Although 19 different sources of stress were identified through the research, Wexler and Logan (1983) assert that the most common were those associated with being female.

In a later study, Wexler (1985) identified female patrol officers using four different role styles and compared these styles to the amount of stress experienced by females. The styles were neutral-impersonal, semi-masculine, feminine, and mixed. She found that the amount of stress these women experience may encourage them to adopt a particular role style. The women who maintained a neutral-impersonal style tended to adopt a rather distant style in order to reduce the amount of stress. Although stress may have been reduced, this also meant that the women had few beneficial experiences with their male counterparts that could also aid in alleviating stress. Women who used the feminine style experienced less stress and frustration at work. Women who had developed a semi-masculine work style experienced the least amount of stress among the women studied. Over half of these women reported experiencing no difficulties with stress at work (Wexler, 1985).

The Wexler (1985) study demonstrates the existence of role conflict for women in nontraditional occupations. Because women are often unwelcome in these traditionally male-dominated environments it is often necessary for them to resolve the problems of their unequal status through role negotiation. Negotiating these roles may result in a greater acceptance of the females by their male counterparts but may also result in increased stress (Wexler, 1985).

Pendergrass and Ostrove (1984) examined both sworn and civilian women's and men's perceptions of stress and related consequences in a Montgomery County, Maryland, police department. Significant differences between women and men include physiological stress consequences, including headaches, muscle tension, nausea/upset stomach, and chest pain/tension. However, women and men did not differ significantly with respect to psychological or behavioral stress consequences, including sleepiness on the job, low self-opinion, insomnia, cynicism, and isolation from coworkers. Additionally, women more often named safety issues as stressful than did men, and men named career issues as stressful more often than did women (Pendergrass and Ostrove, 1984: 307).

Seagram and Stark-Adamec (1992) studied the attrition of female police officers in urban police departments in Canada. Their sample consisted of both current and ex-police officers who were female and male. They investigated stress levels among the officers, coping strategies, and various stress-related complaints. A majority of stressors were given comparable ratings by both male and female officers. There were some differences, however. The female officers identified more stress associated with the assignment of an incompatible partner, delivery of a death notification, and assignment of new or unfamiliar duties; men reported more stress related to political pressure from outside the department, attempts to move up in the organization, and more paperwork (Seagram and Stark-Adamec, 1992: 126). Of particular importance to note is that 18% of the women reported sex-specific problems as having been especially stressful. Sex-specific items include sexual harassment, sex discrimination, pregnancy, and having children while still on the force.

There were quite a few gender differences regarding attrition in this study. Women often cited family-related factors as the primary reason for leaving their jobs. Over half (56%) of the women indicated that their primary reason for leaving was to spend more time with their families and/or raise their children. Only 6% of the women indicated that burnout and negative views about life were the primary reasons for leaving. Men, on the other hand, more frequently indicated that job-related factors were more influential in their leaving the force. Almost half (41%) of the men indicated that their primary reason for leaving was a desire to change occupations or return to school. In stark contrast to the women, over one-fifth (23%) of the men indicated that burnout and negative views about life were their primary reasons for leaving their jobs (Seagram and Stark-Adamec, 1992: 127).

In a longitudinal study, Bartol et al. (1992) examined job performance, self-perceived stress, supervisory-perceived stress, and personality characteristics of police officers in rural Vermont. Eighty-seven stressors were identified in the relevant literature and used to assess stress among the officers. External stressors were found to be the greatest source of stress for both women and men, with organizational stressors following. Overall, women and men experience a majority of similar stressors. However, 53% of the women indicated that they had been sexually harassed while on the job, while 83% felt that male superiors displayed negative attitudes toward them. Female officers experienced more task-related stressors than their male counterparts; for example, females indicated that the tragedy and pain encountered were especially problematic for them. Rumors were also a source of stress for these women.

Morash and Haarr (1995) combined qualitative and quantitative research methods and examined stress in police organizations. Stressors were defined as workplace problems and included those that originate in the structure, climate, and interactions of the workplace. Working with the Police Executive Research Forum (PERF), the researchers identified 24 departments that would participate in the study. Departments ranged in size from 100 to more than 1,000 officers. Geographically, the entire United States area was represented. The researchers indicated, however, that although the sample was varied, it was not representative of the entire law enforcement population. The sample consisted of almost one-third women (30.6%). The women in the sample were younger, had more education, and had fewer years of experience than the men.

Morash and Haarr (1995) used participant observation and in-depth interviews to identify the types and forms of female officers' experiences at work, and their conceptualizations of problems and stresses. With information obtained in observation and interviews, the researchers developed a comprehensive list of women's workplace problems. Using this list (and various analytic techniques), they created scales that served as independent variables in their analysis. This research also used measures that have frequently been used to examine stress in policing, but that have been based primarily on the experiences of white men. The previously mentioned scales are ones that had not been used in other examinations of stress in policing.

Morash and Haarr (1995) identified four problems specific to persons viewed as outsiders or as different from others in the workplace: language harassment, racial/ethnic harassment, stigmatization because of appearance, and the experience of bias and investment of energy to contend with it (p. 123). They found that the strongest predictors of stress for both women and men were lack of influence over daily activities, overestimates of physical abilities, inadequate equipment and uniforms, and lack of advancement opportunities. They also found that two sources of stress, sexual harassment and language harassment, were significantly correlated with workplace problems for women, while men's strongest stressors were being set up in dangerous situations and being ridiculed by coworkers. Morash and Haarr concluded that women face a unique, gender-related set of stressful circumstances, but do not report substantially greater work-related stress than men do (1995: 133).

Haarr and Morash (1999) continued their work and further evaluated stress and coping, and the effects of gender and race on these phenomena. Using a combination of qualitative and quantitative methods, they identified strategies used by police officers to cope with stress in the workplace. A comparison was made for gender and racial groups as related to levels of stress.

Using female-centered research, in which women are the focus of the analyses, Haarr and Morash (1999) combined field research, participant observation, and in-depth interviews of women to identify the types and forms of stress that are found in police work. For this portion of the study, data was collected over a seven-year period in 15 statewide and regional meetings of women in law enforcement.

The qualitative data was then used to create the quantitative measure for the surveys. In collaboration with the Police Executive Research Forum, Haarr and Morash distributed the survey to 2,484 officers in 24 departments that were willing to participate in this project. In the final sample of 1,087 officers, there were 68.6% men and 31.4% women; the group as a whole were primarily Caucasian (78%) with the remaining number African-American (22%).

Haarr and Morash (1999) found that women and men use a wide variety of strategies to deal with stress in the workplace, and that in large degree, they use similar methods of coping. However, they found a significant difference in women and men in the use of psychological escape as a means of coping. Women in this sample used escape more often than men, with those women with higher levels of stress using escape most often. Consistent with other research (Worden, 1993), this suggests that perhaps the effect of the police culture may be more significant than gender in identifying and using coping strategies because of the similarities in findings. Haarr and Morash also found that gender was a significant predictor of levels of stress. The odds of being in a high-stress group increased by 48% if the officer was a woman. They propose that structural and cultural features of police organizations create special problems and pressures for women, which is also consistent with previous research (Haarr, 1997; Hale and Bennett, 1995; Martin, 1980, 1990; Morash and Haarr, 1995; Wexler and Logan, 1983).

Critique of Research

As is evident, research on women in municipal policing is varied and focuses on a wide array of issues. What is problematic in some of the research is that it was designed to evaluate men and cannot adequately evaluate women or women's experiences. Although this is not the case for all of the research, the potential bias of previous research is worth noting. Morash and Greene (1986) assessed the validity of the nine major studies of women on patrol in order to make recommendations for future research and policy recommendations on women and criminal justice. They identified a number of areas in which research on women in policing is gender biased. They found that the evaluations emphasized situations associated most often with males and that the criteria for assessing the officers measured fit with gender stereotypes, and furthermore, that police performance was measured in the context of crime control or some other aspect of police work (Morash and Green, 1986: 234). These evaluations also assumed that observed differences were not a product of negative work experiences. The evaluations also failed to measure the accomplishment of identifiable police tasks (Morash and Green, 1986: 247). They lacked clear standards for weighing frequent police tasks relative to less frequent but critical events and for determining appropriate police performance.

In summary, Morash and Greene (1986) identified the following critical weaknesses in the nine evaluations: (1) the failure of the studies to measure the accomplishment of frequently performed police tasks; (2) the studies stress conformity to male stereotypes; (3) most of the studies did not provide a variety of police activities that were representative of the job as a whole, and instead emphasized more violent or dangerous activities; and (4) most of the studies did not control for differences in assignment or familiarity with (exposure to) different tasks.

Historically, policing has been plagued with a lack of job-relatedness-to-performance evaluations. In other words, officers have been evaluated on tasks that do not accurately depict the nature of police work and the frequency with which these tasks are performed, related to other tasks. According to Morash and Greene (1986), when evaluating officers and examining differences by gender, the accuracy of the evaluations is in further question because not only is the frequency of identified tasks misrepresented, but the tasks that are generally evaluated are those that apply to policing as a masculine occupation.

WOMEN IN PRIVATE SECURITY

Women in private security have only been *described* by empirical means. There has been no evaluative research examining competency or research examining stress. Research is limited to three descriptive works. One study examined private security in St. Louis, Missouri, from 1959 to 1989, and another examined private security in New York City in the 1980s. These were both presented in the Hallcrest II Report (Cunningham, Strauchs, and Van Meter, 1990), which is a descriptive report of the security industry. Finally, a survey of women in security management was conducted through the American Society for Industrial Security (ASIS) (Callan, 1995).

As presented in Hallcrest II, Kakalik and Wildhorn (1972) described the typical security guard as being an aging white male who is poorly educated and poorly paid, is between 40 and 55 years of age, and has little education and only a few years of experience in private security (Cunningham, Strauchs, and Van Meter, 1990: 133). Currently, there is limited data to confirm whether or not this depiction is accurate. According to Cunningham, Strauchs, and Van Meter (1990), most of the descriptions of private security guards come from perceptions, assumptions, and other nonscientific approaches to the issue (Cunningham, Strauchs, and Van Meter, 1990: 138). Unlike public policing with a relative wealth of personnel statistics, private security suffers from a lack of comparable information.

The research that examined private security in St. Louis, Missouri, was a longitudinal study covering three decades and using data from the 1960s, 1970s, and 1980s. Basic demographic data was gathered from security personnel over time and compared. Researchers indicated that the number of women in private security in St. Louis, Missouri, from 1959 to 1989 has doubled every 15 years. Specifically, in 1959, women's representation in private security was practically nonexistent. In 1975, women comprised 7% of the surveyed security force in St. Louis, and by 1989, the percentage of women was 14% (as cited in Cunningham, Strauchs, and Van Meter, 1990: 138). Although the numbers are encouraging at a glance, St. Louis, Missouri, may not be representative of the entire security profession. Furthermore, the only other case study to compare it to is one that was undertaken in New York City in the 1980s. In this research, which also described a surrounding New York City Police Department precinct, women represented 9.3% of the proprietary security force in the Brooklyn neighborhood (n = 54). Women represented 6.4% of the police in the surrounding precinct (as cited in Cunningham, Strauchs, and Van Meter, 1990).

The most current research on women in security management comes from a 1995 work entitled *Women in Security Management: A Status Report*, by J.M. Callan. The paper was based upon a survey of 340 women who were members of the American Society for Industrial Security. They were asked to complete a form designed to measure their attitudes toward their careers in security management. There was a 66.7% response rate with 227 women completing the survey. The survey results provided a profile of women security managers who could be described as follows:

+ Average age of 45 years old
+ Married with children
+ Work for a medium-sized service company
+ Earn on average $49,500 per year
+ Have 13 years in the profession
+ Have been promoted by current employer at least once
+ Hold the title of manager
+ Have experienced gender discrimination.

Callan (1995) indicated that 62% of the respondents had experienced high levels of sex discrimination and at least 50% had experienced sexual harassment. Callan also points out that these high levels of discrimination are consistent with the high numbers of women (63%) in security, agreeing that women in security management are paid less than men for the same work, and that more than half of the respondents believed that their chances for promotion were not as good as their male counterparts. This is consistent with similar studies on male-dominated occupations. For example, in organizations in which the male-dominance model operates, there is a climate of tolerance of sexual harassment (Schein,1994, as cited in Callan). Moreover, according to Thomann and Serritella (1994, as cited in Callan), sexual harassment incidents are significantly higher in male-dominated occupations. Studies also indicated that fewer than 5% of those who experience sexual harassment actually report it, particularly in areas such as law enforcement (Thomann, 1994, as cited by Callan). With regard to the high percentages of women experiencing sexual harassment, Callan notes that in spite of this percentage, overall the women were satisfied with their careers and agreed that women could do well in security.

The educational attainment by the women surveyed in this study is somewhat surprising in that nearly 50% of the respondents did not have a bachelor's degree. This would not be consistent with women in similar management positions or with women in law enforcement. As Forbes, Peircy, and Hayes (1988) concluded, a female may make it to the top with a little formal education in smaller firms, but higher education becomes almost mandatory in the largest firms; 89% have at least an undergraduate degree in the Fortune 500 firms (Forbes, Piercy, and Hayes, 1988).

Therefore, the research raises more questions than it answers with regard to women in the security profession. For example, could the lack of education explain why fewer women are in positions of authority or have such low numbers of representation in professional organizations such as ASIS? Are women being held back, as well as receiving lower salaries, because of their lack of education? And finally, why are women not completing their bachelor of science degrees, and what are the real or perceived barriers for women security professionals in completing their higher education? Clearly, more research is needed in this area.

Comparison with Women in Corrections

Women who work as correctional officers (COs) in prisons are most easily compared to women in private security. In fact with today's move toward privatization in much of corrections, guards are likely to be individuals who work for a contract security company that provides employees to state and federal prisons and local jails. Despite the absence of an examination of women in private security, some valid comparisons may be made between the two occupations for these reasons and the fact that women in both of these professions are in nontraditional occupations for women.

The history of women's representation in corrections has been very similar to that of women in policing. Initially, women were volunteers who were often part of the nineteenth-century Reform Movement and sought to provide assistance to women and children. Women were prohibited from working in institutional corrections that housed both female and male prisoners, and employed individuals were most comparable to a security guard.

In the early 1900s, reformers advocated institutions that housed only women; this soon became a reality for many states (Martin and Jurik, 1996). The establishment of these facilities secured the acceptance of women's appropriateness within institutional corrections. Following this advance, until the 1970s, women worked primarily as administrators, security officers, and counselors in women's facilities, or as probation and parole officers for women and girls. Women, however, were restricted from men's institutions, and therefore could not supervise male inmates (Feinman, 1986). Since the 1970s, due to a variety of legal factors (see Chapter 2), women have participated in all areas of corrections. Interestingly, the area that has been most resistant to the inclusion of women has been security work in men's prisons (Martin and Jurik, 1996: 160).

Morton (1991) indicates that in 1988 women represented approximately 43% of the corrections population, which was comparable to their participation in the workforce at large (Martin and Jurik, 1996). However, women were still working more often in institutions that housed female inmates and were least likely to be found working in maximum security facilities for housing men. Perhaps this fact is due to assumptions that are similar to those found for women in policing with respect to physical abilities: that a more secure facility requires officers who have more physical strength and capabilities. Consequently, men would be more appropriate for jobs in maximum security facilities.

Empirical research evaluating women in corrections has found female correctional security officers to be more educated than their male counterparts (Jurik and Halemba, 1984), and to have been previously employed in traditional occupations for women (Zimmer, 1986). Research also indicates that women were less likely than men to have had previous law enforcement experience than their male counterparts (Jurik and Halemba, 1984; Zimmer, 1986). When compared to public law enforcement, there appears to be a higher representation of women of color in corrections (Martin and Jurik, 1996).

Although a great deal of research has been done on women in municipal policing, some of the work still suffers from inherent bias, due to the fact that the design was male-centered, focusing solely or primarily on men. Research on women in private security is almost nonexistent, and what is available is limited. It may be possible to draw on what we have learned about women in policing and corrections to begin to examine women in private security. It is imperative, however, to continue to examine women's role in law enforcement using an approach that adequately assesses both women's and men's experience, to provide the best picture of workers in these organizations. Quality research can provide valuable information to those in decision-making positions in law enforcement organizations who have the potential to make work more satisfying, organizations more efficient, and, ultimately, opportunities equal.

6

Women Executives

This chapter provides an overview of women's positions in management. Leadership styles are discussed and comparisons are made with male counterparts. Although research reveals that there are notable differences in how women and men lead, fundamentally there are fewer and fewer differences in key management traits. The lines between male and female management styles/traits are blurred more now than they have ever been, with the most significant differences existing between transactional and transformational leadership styles. These leadership styles, which are typically observed within a private or corporate structure, also manifest themselves within law enforcement organizations. Not surprisingly, both women and men in law enforcement leadership positions exhibit gender- and non-gender-specific management traits. Also, both women and men identify stress associated from these types of demanding executive positions.

CURRENT STATUS OF WOMEN EXECUTIVES

According to an issue of *Working Woman* (Cleaver, 2000), "companies are more results-oriented than ever in their efforts to recruit and retain female executives" (p. 51). Moreover, they suggest that leadership development programs are becoming more and more popular and have been found to be effective in enhancing the status of women executives. In a 1999 survey of Fortune 500 human resource executives by the Society for Human Resource Management, 85% of respondents said they saw increased opportunities for women. Although women have made significant strides in both the private and public sectors, they still lag behind in the upper management of these agencies. For example, in the private sector, women make up 71% of managers but only account for 42% of senior corporate officers. Women in public law enforcement have experienced similar advancements. Private security, however, appears to be making greater use of women than public law enforcement. For example, according to the Hallcrest Report, 6% of public law enforcement officers are female as compared to 24% of the employees in proprietary companies and 12% in contractual companies (Collins, Ricks, and Van Meter, 2000). Unfortunately, women's inclusion in the rank and file has not necessarily resulted in gender equity at the executive levels.

WOMEN EXECUTIVES AND LEADERSHIP STYLES

Women's leadership styles have been compared to men's in numerous studies, all of which agree that there are marked differences. One of the more recent works on women's leadership styles was that of Helgesen (1995) in her book the *Web of Inclusion*. She describes this web as having leaders that are more comfortable being in the center of things rather than at the top and who prefer building consensus to issuing orders. Women tended to put themselves at the centers of their organizations rather than at the top, and they labored constantly to include people in their decision-making (Helgesen, 1995: 10). In comparison, men's leadership styles are clearly different from women's. Through early work done by Mintzberg (1973) in his research on male managers, we have come to learn much about the male leadership model. He was interested in learning what it is that men do as leaders within an organization on a daily basis. He found that male managers spend more than half of their working day in formal scheduled meetings. The rest of the day was spent in rushed meetings with clients, staff, and others. A typical day could be described as consisting of interruptions, discontinuity, and fragmentation. In other words, men were performing crisis management or putting out fires (Mintzberg, 1973: 29).

Generally, the male managers had little time for activities not directly related to their work. Although men are credited with placing greater emphasis on family relations and even occasionally take advantage of maternity leave programs, in Mintzberg's study, family was secondary to their careers. He described these men as being in intellectual isolation with a deep but narrow focus (Mintzberg, 1973: 30).

Male managers preferred face-to-face meetings for gaining information and often avoided mail or paper forms of communication. One may conclude that with the advent of E-mail, men would be more likely to gravitate to this form of communication because the use of technology allows them to communicate in a paperless format and what could be referred to as a virtual face-to-face dialog. However, a top NBC executive responsible for selling ads for the network's international cable properties admits that he has little knowledge of the Internet and rarely uses the computer in his office at NBC. It is ironic that in his position of international marketing and with the importance of technology to his profession he is not that familiar with the application and uses of technology. As an executive, some 30 years after Mintzberg's original study, this NBC executive more closely resembles his contemporaries who Mintzberg described as being very adept at maintaining a complex network of relationships with people outside their organizations, and who spent little time on correspondence, mail, or other similar activities.

Following Mintzberg's work, Helgesen (1990) found some interesting contrasts between women and men in her work on women's leadership styles. According to Helgesen, women tend to incorporate small breaks throughout the day, scheduling time for themselves, such as arriving the night before a meeting. Women also tended to make time for activities not directly related to their work, with family taking great priority. Helgesen also identified the following leadership styles of the women she interviewed:

1. Women preferred live-action encounters, but also scheduled time to attend to mail. Although they were similar with Mintzberg's men in that they preferred to deal with people in brief, on the phone, they did not view the mail as a burden. They also worked to keep relationships in good repair.
2. They maintained a complex network of relationships with people outside their organizations. They also spent 20 to 40% of their time with clients, peers, and colleagues.
3. Women tended to take a more philosophical view of their personal leadership styles, paying greater attention to long-range planning, while men were more focused on day-to-day tasks of management.
4. Women saw their own identities as complex and multifaceted and demonstrated greater flexibility in their leadership role.
5. Women were better at sharing information, which in part was attributed to the structure of their organizations, which tended to be networks or grids rather than traditional hierarchies (Helgesen, 1995a).

It appears that women and men have strengths in different areas, thereby making each more effective at certain tasks. The challenge, then, is to identify areas in which people excel and assign them to best fit the organizational needs based upon their strengths and not their gender.

A number of studies have been done that identify successful traits of male and female managers. The following discussion represents a summary of some of the major findings. According to Rosen and Jerdee (1978), women were seen less favorably in terms of the knowledge, aptitudes, skills, motivation, interests, temperament, and work habits that are demanded in most managerial roles. Although somewhat counterintuitive, older male managers who were more likely to have worked with a female manager were found to be less traditional in their perceptions of women than their younger colleagues (Massengill and DiMarco, 1979). In other words, men who have had experience working with women had favorable impressions of them. Additionally, women who prefer to be addressed with Ms. had a better chance of being seen as a successful manager than women who chose more traditional forms of address (Dion and Schuller, 1990).

Donnell and Hall (1980) found differences on two minor variables in their extensive study of female and male managers: women scored high on social and work incentives and men on interpersonal competence between managers and their peers, which would suggest that women are more motivated by such intrinsic rewards as establishing good relations with coworkers, whereas men find greater satisfaction in being seen as competent by their peers. In groups where no leader is designated, men will emerge as leaders more frequently than women. This could be attributed to a number of factors, one of which is women's tendency to share power more easily than men. The qualities most frequently found among emergent leaders are dominance, intelligence, and both masculinity and femininity (Dobbins, 1990).

In the book *The Managerial Woman* by Hennig and Jardin (1977), the life experiences of 25 top-level women managers were compared. The focus of the study was how these women managed to depart from traditional female roles to achieve success in a man's world. The factors that distinguished successful women managers in this study were:

1. All 25 managers were first-born and were either an only child or the eldest in an all-girl family of no more than three children;
2. Each identified more with her father and received support and encouragement to succeed;
3. All of the women had attended college and completed their degrees;
4. They spent their entire career at one firm;

5. None of the women managers married before age 35 and none had children;
6. All of the women reported having a male mentor;
7. All were born during the period in which the first women's movement was at its height;
8. Much of their early career programs took place during World War II when a shortage of male workers created greater opportunities for women.

Hennig and Jardin (1977) assert that it is difficult to conclude whether the success of these women was due to their managerial traits or that they reached career maturity at a unique time.

The success of these early women managers rested on their ability to mask their feminine traits and mimic their male counterparts. They had to forego their personal lives and resign themselves to the fact that the organization was their family. The more successful they were at concealing any gender differences, the more successful they became at assimilating into the male-dominated professions.

Research by Rosener (1990) focused upon the unique differences that are manifested in male and female leadership styles. She describes their differences as being either transactional leadership or transformational leadership. The men in her study tended to use transactional leadership, while the women tended to use transformational leadership more often. Transactional leadership comes from organizational position. Consequently, because men generally have higher organizational positions, it is logical that their leadership styles would support their maintaining these organizational positions. Women, on the other hand, use transformational leadership, which relates to transforming one's own self-interest into the interest of the group or greater goal. One could speculate that because women have not historically been in positions of power they have developed other skills that rely more on building relationships rather than relying on the power inherent in certain positions. Rosener's study also confirmed similar research that showed that women tend to encourage greater participation and share power and information more readily than men.

Often useful to understanding female leadership styles is the comparison of women in nontraditional occupations (20% or fewer females) to women in more traditional professions such as nursing. Based upon a study by Moore and Rickel (1980), nontraditional women were more achieving, emphasized production more, and saw themselves as having characteristics more like managers and men. Moore and Rickel found that businesswomen considered the domestic role less important and tended to have fewer children. Effective women managers differed very little from effective men managers in terms of their attitudes, motivation, and behavior. Moreover, Moore and Rickel concluded that traits that are perceived as being related to managerial success and policing generally are ones that are also perceived as masculine.

In a study that focuses more specifically on law enforcement, Price (1974) administered a general personality test to Pennsylvania police officers in order to determine whether or not discernable leadership traits could be identified among police executives. Although this leadership inventory did not measure police performance skills, it did examine the leadership characteristics of women police in these urban police departments. The personality test, designed by a criminologist-psychologist, provided a general picture of personality organization. It consisted of a list of 325 randomly ordered items to which the subject reacted. Depending upon how the subject responded, a specific scale measuring a personality trait would be calculated. This trait-specific study recognized the small number of women executives studied as a limitation that was nonetheless unavoidable, because of the lack of women in executive-level positions.

Price compared leadership traits of men and women police executives, looking specifically at whether or not women exhibit stronger, weaker, or the same leadership traits as men and what, if any, general personality traits are significantly different between the two. The results suggest that women tend to exhibit greater leadership strength in areas of conservatism, which measures the level of flexibility and the tendency to stick to routine and convention. Therefore, women tend to be more flexible and prone to taking a problem-solving approach to complex issues or unique situations. Men tended to score higher than females on persistence, which measures an individual's ability to stay focused on a particular issue or activity, even in the face of difficulties or opposition. Women scored slightly higher than men in the area of initiative, which referred to the tendency to plan, manage, and organize. What is even more interesting is where there were very few, if any, significant differences between men and women. For example, there were no differences between the two in oral skills, ambition, or competitiveness.

Price's study represents one of the first studies to focus on female police executives. Her study came on the heels of significant changes that had taken place in police procedures, such as the elimination of special women's units and the relaxation of height, weight, and special education entrance requirements for women. Most would agree that changes in the laws made such access to nontraditional occupations for women possible in the 1970s. However, some veteran preference systems, which give credit for military service, still operate and, in practice, are discriminatory against females. It is still too early to assess what the long-term effect such policies may have on the current status of women and the future recruitment of women and minorities—and, consequently, on opportunities for women executives.

A study of women chiefs of police by Stickely (1987) provides a basis on which to compare the advancement of women law enforcement executives. It also provides data on women in rural and small town law enforcement agencies. At the time of her study there were only about 30 women chiefs, and she obtained information from 11 of them. These women had served from almost two years to seven and one-half years in small departments, ranging in size from 4 to 28 sworn officers. The communities these women served ranged in population from approximately 450 to 35,000 citizens. Most of the women were political appointees (Stickley, as cited in Lunnenborg,

1989). Stickley identified six factors that the chiefs felt had helped them in achieving their position:

1. Previous experience in all phases of police work is most important.
2. Education is also crucial.
3. Superior performance is necessary. Women have to be quicker, sharper, more understanding, more mature, more innovative, and more enthusiastic about police work.
4. Goal setting and determination to reach goals are essential.
5. Community involvement is recommended. Volunteer work related to police work is another way of getting training. Visibility strengthens support from others (Stickley, 1989).

PROFILES OF WOMEN EXECUTIVES IN LAW ENFORCEMENT

Research on women executives parallels other research on women in policing in that women are generally found to be competent and capable, but they still meet with resistance, as evidenced by Gold's (1999) work on women executives in law enforcement. Gold interviewed 13 women in law enforcement command positions, including lieutenants, captains, sheriffs, and chiefs. The careers of these women span three decades and provide a rich documentation of their shared experiences in advancing within the ranks to top command positions. Table 6.1 details each of the women's rank, position, education, and years of service, and her perspective on whether or not she believed that her gender had an effect on advancement.

There are a number of interesting points to make regarding the 13 top law enforcement executives that Gold interviewed. First of all, each of the women represented worked for medium to large agencies. Of the 13 officers interviewed, only two women held the top executive position of their agencies. As the size of the agency increased, there was an inverse relation to the number of women in top command positions. This is surprising because one might assume

Table 6.1   Women's rank, position, education, years of service, and gender effect on advancement.

Agency	Rank	Position	Education (*FBI Academy)	Years of Service	Agency Data (% of Women Officers/% of Women in Top Command)	Gender Effect on Advancement
St. Paul, MN, Police Dept.	Lieutenant	Foot Patrol Division	Associate Degree *FBI	19	13.5% Women/ 14% Top Command	No
N.Y. State Police	Captain	Training	Bachelor's Degree	15	8% Women/ 3.7% Top Command	No
Co. Sheriff Seattle, WA	Major	Precinct	Bachelor's Degree *FBI	21	17% Women/ 28% Top Command	Yes
Phoenix Police Dept.	Commander	Planning & Research	Master's Degree	18	10.7% Women/ 11% Top Command	No
Co. Sheriff Travis, TX	Sheriff	Sheriff	Juris Doctorate Degree	25	19% Women/ 36% Top Command	No

Portland OR, Police Dept.	Chief of Police	Chief of Police	Bachelor's Degree	22	17% Women/ 11% Top Command	Yes
Tulsa, OK, Police Dept.	Major	Patrol	Master's Degree *FBI	28	14% Women/ 8.6% Top Command	Yes
Los Angeles Police Dept.	Asst. Commander	Operations	Juris Doctorate Degree	20	17% Women/ 3.3% Top Command	Yes
Illinois State Police	Deputy Director	Forensic Services	Bachelor's Degree *FBI	24	9% Women/ 11% Top Command	Yes
Co. Sheriff Phoenix, AZ	Lieutenant	Chief of Police Services	Unknown	18	7% Women/ 5% Top Command	No
Co. Sheriff Phoenix, AZ	Chief Deputy	Chief Deputy	Bachelor's Degree *FBI	25	7% Women/ 5% Top Command	No
Chicago Police Dept.	District Commander	District	Master's Degree	23	19% Women/ 5% Top Command	No

that the larger the agency the larger the pool of women to select from, and the greater the opportunity for advancement of women. But based upon Gold's study, in the two largest agencies, Chicago and Los Angeles, women in top command were only 5% and 3.3%, respectively. One could speculate that as the agency size increased so did the competition for these positions, for both the female and male officers.

For men, attendance at the FBI Academy leadership program is almost a prerequisite to advancement in their organization. These are highly sought after seats and availability is limited. Of the women interviewed in this study, only four attended the Academy, and their current rank varied from Lieutenant to Chief Deputy. It is unclear as to whether there is any correlation to attending the FBI academy and promotion. Of those four, all but one of the women had some level of higher education and two of the women had law degrees. Of the two officers with law degrees, both held a high command position, a Deputy Commander and a sheriff.

Traditionally, women have been given positions within law enforcement that are considered more appropriate for females, such as working with children or women. However, it would appear from Gold's study that the majority of the women were in traditional law enforcement positions.

When asked if they felt that their gender affected their advancement, both negatively and/or positively, the results were mixed. Seven of the 13 women interviewed felt that their gender had very little to do with their advancement within the organization. One woman in particular felt that her small size had more of a negative impact on her advancement than the fact that she was female. Many of the women indicated that they did not feel their gender had an impact on promotions and believed that their determination and hard work are what contributed to their advancement within the organization. The only female sheriff had this to say about her advancement within the agency: "Gender became a non-issue when people realized they were not going to scare me off" (Gold, 1999: 87).

The women who indicated that gender did affect their advancement had both positive and negative experiences. In fact, some negative experiences had to be overcome in order to break through the glass ceiling of promotion. Only two of the 13 women relied upon legal means to resolve what they believed to be discriminatory practices. Of these two women, one ultimately rose to the top of her agency when she became the first chief of police of a large metropolitan police organization, only to be toppled just a year and a half into her tenure due to controversy and political differences. Over the course of her 22-year career with this police agency, she filed 42 civil rights complaints and numerous discrimination complaints against the department. It would appear that although she paved the way for women police officers, she paid a heavy price for her efforts. Of the 40 or more lawsuits, none ended in an award or in her favor. The other officer filed a class action lawsuit because of lower salaries for the women police officers in her force as compared to the male police officers. Her legal action had a more positive ending, resulting in a promotion and pay raise to detective.

Most of the women in this study had aspirations for promotion. Only four of the women had no thoughts of seeking advancement, with some even planning on staying with the police department just long enough to find other employment. All of the women spoke highly of the importance of networking and their affiliation with professional police organizations, such as the National Association of Women Law Enforcement Executives.

The most current research on women executives comes from the National Center for Women and Policing and the International Association of Chiefs of Police. Both surveys found that women in executive law enforcement positions (top command) are estimated at approximately 5.6% of the total executive level positions in law enforcement (NCWP, 2000). It is somewhat disconcerting that both studies show that a significant number of agencies continue to report a lack of women in top command positions.

WOMEN EXECUTIVES AND STRESS

Christophe (1988) described women executives' attempts at managing androgynously, with no definite masculine or feminine characteristics, and the stress associated with this style. This is similar to

Martin's (1980) description of women in policing negotiating their roles through being either Police women or police Women. Christophe identified a five-stage process that women executives undertake in attempting to create a work environment in which women and men engage in consciously satisfactory behavior in their working relationships (Christophe, as cited in Lunnenborg, 1989: 98). In Phase One, these women are aware of the unconscious, unsatisfactory, sexist behavior (p. 97) that many men display toward women; the stress of this realization results in fatigue and depression for the women. Although most women tend to use different styles depending on the circumstance, and generally fall somewhere in between, it is important to note the existence of role negotiation, or attempting to decide what is most "appropriate" in a given situation. The fact that women must do this to be accepted in their positions as police officers reflects the complexities of participating in such masculine-defined occupations.

In Phase Two, executive women watch typical sex role behaviors from the men, and perceive that no one besides themselves cares about the behavior. In Phase Three, the women project their frustration toward the men, which in turn causes them to be more aggressive and hostile. In Phase Four, the men who are engaging in this conscious sexist behavior want relationships to be governed by the old familiar rules of traditional sex roles (Lunnenborg, 1989: 97).

Christophe (1988) advises women in this Phase Four to seek counsel from other women. In Phase Five, it is hoped that both women and men are no longer engaging in sexist behavior, at which time women executives can concentrate on making necessary changes in the organization to better the organization and prevent the reoccurrence of unwanted sexist behavior. In Phase Five, the woman executive's stress level decreases because she is free to use the complementary traits of both sexes to manage in a truly androgynous mode (Lunnenborg, 1989: 98).

The evolution of these phases is best illustrated by the following situation in which the first woman Lt. Commander in the Los Angeles Police Department described an early experience in her career when she confronted an adversarial colleague who created an intolerable work environment for her and other women. A fellow male detective would degrade her in front of others and refused to work with her on assignments. After approaching her supervisor and being told that she ought to be wearing certain types of clothes and she ought to be home cooking for her husband, she decided to deal with the situation herself. The following is her account of how she dealt with the situation in a private conversation she had with the fellow officer:

You got a lot of time on the job. I would call you one of the department's dinosaurs, and I'm just a young kid. You can make me or you can break me, and you're just about ready to break me . . . I'm just about there. I can't do this anymore. I can't survive in this. I don't like it. I don't like you. I don't like what I'm doing. I don't like myself right now. But, I'm really, really smart. I can do this stuff. I catch on really quick. I learn really fast. I can be a great detective. But, I can't do it alone. So you can do one of two things . . . You can either break me, and then you can tell everybody how you broke that young little girl and made her go away. Or, you can teach me everything you know, and then someday I'm going to be somebody, and you can say you taught me. Now, you do one or the other. I'll go away, and it's not going to be good, and you know it might hurt you somewhere down the line, or I can be your protégé. What do you want to do?

The male officer decided, after much discussion, that he would work with her. As she predicted, he now works *for* her and they have a good working relationship.

How can agencies improve their organizations and create an atmosphere that not only attracts but also retains women police managers? There may be some answers from programs that are currently being used in the private sector. For example, one Fortune 500 Corporation developed a leadership program nearly 20 years ago that created a system that allowed for the advancement of women executives. The program was referred to as the Organizational and Management Development Review Program (OMDR). Part of its mission was an initiative to accelerate the advancement of women and minorities in the organization. Early on in the process the company adopted parity goals, which established a goal of promoting at least three women and minorities to vice president. These individuals were identified through a leadership system and referred to as high potentials. Evaluation forms were sent out to each of the organization's major divisions. Division managers were then required to identify four categories of high potential employees: white men, women, minorities, and technical staff. Each division manager had to include career development plans for each of the high potential individuals. These career plans included such things as developmental rotations, which required the employee to work in different areas to become more knowledgeable about the company and its various divisions. The division recommendations were then returned to corporate management who selected at least three women and minorities for vice president positions. The leadership program in this organization has been successful, as evidenced by the fact that more than 40 female vice presidents, 7 of whom are women of color, are currently in the position of vice president. Similar organizations demonstrating success in recruiting, retention, and promotion of women and minorities have a number of things in common:

+ Formal leadership program
+ Commitment to advancing women and minorities
+ Identifiable goals by which to measure success

Although this is an example that comes from the private sector, there are elements that would certainly be transferable to public law enforcement.

POTENTIAL OPPORTUNITIES FOR WOMEN EXECUTIVES

Couper and Lobitz (1988) propose that the quality and productivity movement that has transformed business is influencing policing. This is seen in the community oriented policing (COP) model which they described as policing that is more service oriented, requiring a new style of leadership. The new style of leadership appropriate for this model advocates the use of teamwork, a focus on customer needs, asking and listening to employees, bosses working as coaches and teachers, trusting employees, and examining errors from a systems perspective to evaluate processes that need improvement. Obviously, COP is significantly different than the traditional professional model that is characterized by a rigid bureaucratic hierarchy, placing value on traits identified as inherently masculine, such as aggression. Lunnenborg asserts, too, that if the movement towards quality and productivity in policing is real, then women should be further considered for administrative and managerial positions, while testing previous assumptions that men prefer top-down, power-oriented leadership with little focus on the customer or employee (Lunnenborg, 1989: 184). Implications of this shift and the effect of COP on the police organization, potentially creating new opportunities for women, will be discussed further in Chapter 7.

7

Special Issues

Numerous issues could potentially be special issues for women in law enforcement today. Based on research to date, anecdotal evidence, and in consideration of the anticipated needs of women in law enforcement in the next century, this chapter examines contemporary issues using a multiple levels approach: individual, organizational, and societal. The current status of women, community oriented policing, and mentoring and networking have been chosen as the focal points. Mentoring and networking will be examined at the individual level; community oriented policing will be examined at the organizational level; and the increased status of women will be examined at the societal level.

CURRENT STATUS OF WOMEN

American women tend to be more educated than their male counterparts, obtaining 50% of all the bachelor and master's of science degrees. Women, for the first time in the history of the United States, represent the largest national economy on earth (Peters, 1999: 399). Some of the latest statistics with regard to women are startling:

10.2 million women (20% of working wives) earn more than their husbands.

Women represent 45% of Americans with assets greater than $500,000.

Women make 85% of the purchasing decisions in the following areas: home furnishings, holidays, homes, bank accounts, and medical insurance.

Women make 65% of car-buying decisions.

Women have established a strong economic voice. According to Elissa Moses of the BrainWave Group, a market research firm in New York, the women's movement in the 1990s has become the pursuit of self-navigation, meaning a search for equality, with distinctions between the sexes. Women are more interested in financial independence and control over their lives and working circumstances. They also want to stay open to possibilities and are flexible; they want balance in their careers; and they are in search of pleasure and enjoyment and are taking responsibility for themselves (Peters, 1994).

Because of the glass ceiling that women have bumped up against continually in both the public and private sectors, they have had to approach opportunity and career development creatively. According to the National Federation of Independent Business there are approximately 9 million businesses (38%) owned by women. The growth has been in nontraditional areas for women such as manufacturing, construction, and wholesale distribution.

WOMEN IN NONTRADITIONAL CAREERS

Women who have pursued nontraditional professions, such as law enforcement, have often done so to compete for greater earning potential. By breaking down some of these barriers women have greater access to nontraditional careers or opportunities, especially in white-collar professions such as medicine, law, or finance. For example, the 1996 class entering Yale Medical School was 54% female. Although white-collar opportunities have increased for women, many of the nontraditional blue-collar positions, such as the trades and law enforcement, continue to remain male bastions. Women still continue to be underrepresented in these areas.

Some would suggest that women are simply not interested in these types of positions, and with greater opportunity in other areas of work the numbers of women interested in police work, for example, are much less. However, according to Donna Milgram, Executive Director of the Institute for Women in Trades, Technology, and the Sciences (IWITTS), the fact that nationally only 10% to 12% of police officers are women does not adequately explain why there are greater percentages of female police officers in departments such as Tucson, Arizona (29%), Miami Beach, Florida (28%), Madison, Wisconsin (26%), Pittsburgh, Pennsylvania (22%), and Birmingham, Alabama (19%). Milgram suggests that it is not an issue of interest but rather an issue of recruitment, pointing to the fact that the Tucson Police Department was able to increase its numbers of women police officers from 10% to 29% by changing the way in which women were recruited to the department. For example, many of these departments hosted Women and Policing Career Fairs that used the media to promote the event; developed fliers, posters, and brochures featuring female officers; and created a targeted recruitment list.

COMMUNITY ORIENTED POLICING

One of the barriers identified by the National Center for Women and Policing in its second annual national status report on women in policing was the outdated model of policing that is currently utilized in many of today's departments. It describes this model as being a paramilitaristic one that rewards tough, aggressive, even violent behavior and that results in poor community relations, increased citizen complaints, and more violent confrontations and deaths (NCWP, 1999: 4). Furthermore, the Center maintains that by adopting a community oriented policing model more women could possibly be attracted to the profession.

Community oriented policing (COP) has changed the face of contemporary American policing. Unlike the traditional professional model of policing that emphasizes a rigid bureaucratic chain of command with limited challenges and opportunities for professional development, COP advocates a model that encourages officer creativity and ingenuity and operates with a much more fluid organizational structure. Although there are only estimations of how many organizations define themselves as following a COP model, a substantial number of organizations have indicated their adoption and support of this new form of policing.

When organizations adopt COP as their philosophical and operational approach to policing, this changes virtually everything about the organization, from recruiting strategies to methods of employee evaluation. An organization's mission statement, goals, and objectives are typically changed as well. A change from a traditional professional model of policing to a COP model could have numerous implications for not only the community that is being served, but also employees within the organization. Specifically, when the organizational structure, resource management, and police operations are transformed, numerous opportunities for women may exist that have been virtually unavailable until the adoption of COP.

To understand the significance of the transformation, the two models must be compared. The traditional professional model, which has dominated policing for the last three decades, has been described as a bureaucratic efficiency model that values behaviors that have typically been described as masculine in nature and have supported the professional model to its fullest extent.

Thorough research examining gender and community policing is limited with one exception. Using both quantitative and qualitative methods, Miller (1999) conducted a comprehensive analysis of gender and community policing in a small Midwestern town using a triangulated method to gather data, including field observation, survey research, and in-depth interviews. The sample of 65 officers of the Jackson City police department consisted of 45 current or former neighborhood police officers (NPO), 19 patrol officers, and 6 key administrators. NPOs were the officers performing COP, while the patrol officers typically reacted to calls for service in their assigned neighborhoods. By looking at a department having both the NPOs and the patrol officers, Miller was able to compare the traditional and COP models.

Miller developed an original framework for this analysis and asked fundamental questions that must be answered to fully understand the complexities of the argument:

(1) How can policing with its paramilitary and masculinist structure be transformed to honor the values of care, connection, empathy, and informality?
(2) What changes must occur to reconcile the contradictions between "masculine" and "feminine" police activities?
(3) What matters more, the gender of the officers, or that officers of either gender actively integrate "feminine" traits into their social control and policing ideology?
(4) Will male and female officers be evaluated differently because of gender-based assumptions? (Miller, 1999: 68)

What Miller forces the reader to do is ask whether resistance to community policing is resistance to the task of policing, or whether the resistance is actually nothing more than resistance to a new way of "gendering" the organization into one that values traditionally feminine characteristics.

Miller found that in the early stages of the department's utilization of NPOs, primarily women and men of color applied for these positions and consequently got them. After it appeared that NPOs fared better with respect to promotion than non-NPOs, white males started applying for the positions.

Most NPOs reported difficulty making a transition from the reactive traditional patrol to the more proactive, citizen-focused neighborhood patrol. New NPOs still emphasized the crime-fighting nature of their work, while slowly developing skills and resources more characteristic of the service or social work emphases of neighborhood policing (Miller, 1999). According to Miller, male officers indicated that neighborhood policing provided them with opportunities to develop their interpersonal communications skills (p. 123).

In contrast, the traditional patrol officers described their work as lacking any social work activities and not requiring continued dialogue with the community, as did the NPOs' job.

In another work, Delong (1997) examined two police agencies, one that operated under a traditional model and one that had adopted COP as an organizational philosophy. Delong hypothesized that the COP organization's employees were more likely than the traditional organization's employees to have positive attitudes toward women in policing. She found that women were perceived by those in the COP organization more positively than officers in the traditional organization, and more specifically that men in both organizations had more negative views of women in policing than did women in both organizations (Delong, 1997).

MENTORING AND NETWORKING

Mentoring

Research has shown a direct relationship between mentoring and men's and women's success and satisfaction with their careers. Career-related mentoring can involve a combination of the following roles by the mentor or sponsor:

Teacher: Enhancing the young person's skills and intellectual development; giving feedback on performance; teaching tricks of the trade; and socializing the protégé to value differences within the organization (Kram and Parker, 1993).

Sponsor: Using his/her influence to facilitate the younger person's entry and advancement; fighting for the protégé by standing up for her/him in meetings if controversy arises; promoting his/her candidacy for promising opportunities and challenging assignments; publicizing accomplishments; providing reflected power and putting the resources of the sponsor behind the protégé; and providing exposure and visibility as well as protection (Kram, 1983).

Host and guide: Welcoming the initiate into a new occupational and social world and acquainting him/her with its values, customs, resources, and cast of characters; giving maximum responsibility and exposure to new functional areas; bypassing the hierarchy by getting inside information or shortcutting cumbersome procedures or red tape (Kanter, 1977).

Mentoring has been described as requiring a position of power. Those persons who can identify and sponsor potential future leaders of an organization are not without influence and positions of authority themselves, which may provide some of the explanation as to why so few women serve as mentors.

Although it seems logical that women could and would want to mentor other women, especially when they achieve positions of authority, this is not always the case. In some cases, women who are potential mentors for less experienced and oftentimes subordinate women are reluctant to establish relationships. They become aloof and make themselves inaccessible. This phenomenon is known as the Queen Bee syndrome (Staines, Tavris, and Jayaratne, 1974; Yoder, Adams, Grove, and Priest, 1985). The primary reason for women developing this style is for protection. These women enjoy their status as decision-makers, and they want to maintain that status out of self-interest (Staines et al., 1974). It appears that they may not want to risk assisting other women for fear that they may achieve more than they themselves have. In a study of women at the U.S. Military Academy at West Point, Yoder and her colleagues (1985) found that upper-class women in particular exhibited Queen Bee behavior. The upper-class women would not associate with under-class women, unless it was a function involving sports. Furthermore, the upper-class women indicated that it was they who shunned sponsorship rather than the failure of the new cadets to seek them (Yoder et al., 1985: 125).

Roche (1979) indicated that professional women have mentors, but they are rarely women. Also, the mentors oftentimes did not work in the same organization. Surprisingly, however, women often have more mentors than men. This phenomenon appears to be consistent over at least the last 25 years, as indicated by Roche's work in 1979 in which women average three sponsors or mentors to men's two. Very similar statistics have emerged from research conducted by the Institute for Women in Technology, Trades and Sciences (IWITTS) in which more women police officers (60%) in two medium-sized departments indicated they had mentors more than their male (38%) counterparts (Polisar and Milgram, 1998).

Mentoring was also listed as an important source of assistance in professional development. According to a study by Callan (1995) examining attitudes of women security managers, 58% of respondents indicated that they had a mentor during their careers in security management, and 77% of the women agreed that they would serve as mentors to other women in security.

As will be noted in Chapter 9, which contains interviews with women in law enforcement today, most of the respondents indicated that they had mentors, and most of these mentors were male. Most of the respondents were between 35 and 54 years of age, and averaged 18 years of service in their professions. The fact that most of the women had almost 20 years in their chosen careers means that most of them entered their careers in the mid to late seventies, when the representation of women in law enforcement was at about 6%. Consequently, there were very few women in positions of authority who could have been role models. Mentors may be those who are similarly situated in an organization, but it appears to make a difference to individuals who are mentored if their mentors are like them with respect to gender. If a woman sees the successes of another woman, it may perhaps give her the incentive to pursue promotion in her organization.

Limited numbers of law enforcement organizations have formal mentoring programs, whether in policing or private security. Mentoring advocates suggest that more formalized programs may be useful to both women and men. Employers would be advised to go beyond traditional practices of informal mentoring and pursue formal programs that might make their employees more effective and satisfied employees.

Why is there a need for women to mentor other women? Duff (1999) indicates that men can also be wonderful career mentors for women, but because men haven't shared the same experiences as women, they cannot redefine and redesign the workplace to reflect individual values and support the professional development like women can (Duff, 1999: xiv). Also, when women are mentored by women in senior positions, this indicates that senior decision-making positions are attainable, and that gender does not hinder success and promotion in the organization (Ely, as cited in Duff,' 1999: 25).

Women mentoring women in the workplace is described as a contemporary phenomenon. These relationships include circumstances and rules that are specific to a female style and representative of a female culture (Duff, 1999: xv).

Duff (1999) indicates that other women in your profession offer gold to be mined (p. 29). However, in order to enrich mentoring relationships, certain myths must be debunked. These include the myth that you will be rejected, the myth that women owe you something, the myth of the Dead Even rule, the myth of the Queen Bee, the myth of the Destructive Woman, and other Women-Can't-Work-With-Women Stereotypes (Duff, 1999).

Many women may forego mentoring relationships to avoid being rejected by someone from whom they believe they may be able to learn. Opportunities to mentor may be declined on occasion, but more often they are not declined. It is important to realize that a declination of a mentoring relationship should not be taken personally. It is possible that the prospective mentor may have made her decision because of situational politics or lack of time, and not the lack of potential in the protégé (Duff, 1999).

Some women assume that they have the right to be mentored by other women simply because they are women, or that other women "owe them something" (Duff, 1999: 18). These women are described as being self-centered and potentially disrespectful. What is also problematic is that they often feel that they have to leave the organization that they work for to be more successful, instead of remaining in the same organization and being successful. This may put women in positions in which they will withhold what they could share if they feel they are being used for their accomplishments rather than appreciated for their abilities and recognized for the dedication and the struggle that led to their achievements (Duff, 1999: 19).

Duff, quoting Heim in *Hardball for Women*, indicates that the dead even rule has women attacking and diminishing the achievements that put one woman ahead of another so that women can feel comfortable with their sameness (p. 20). In other words, instead of women capitalizing on their differences and learning from each other, women may feel threatened if one has accomplishments unlike their own; if the accomplishments are different, the differences could be construed as threatening. Whether differences are minimal or great, Duff emphasizes that any exchange of information can be beneficial to both parties.

Although Queen Bees may be the exception and not the rule, their existence or effects may be problematic (Duff, 1999). These are women who have staked out their territory and have become defensive and protective if any other woman comes close (p. 21). In some cases, women who are not Queen Bees appear to be because they are extremely busy, protective of their time and energy, and resentful of women who imposed on them with demands for special attentions they had never encouraged (p. 22). Women may be misunderstood under these circumstances, which may result in both the suspect Queen Bee and the woman hoping to be mentored losing out on a valuable relationship. As is evident in this situation, the importance of clear communication in potential mentoring relationships cannot be overstated.

Developing a beneficial mentoring relationship cannot be undertaken without first eliminating stereotypes and their effects. The myth of the Destructive Woman and Other-Women-Can't-Work-With-Women Stereotypes exist today in large part due to women's confused expectations concerning the ways in which women relate to one another at home and in our communities and how we must conduct ourselves in order to be effective both professionally and personally (Duff, 1999: 23). Furthermore, when women appear to be intently focused on the bottom line and not attending to the emotional needs of employees instead, the myth of the Destructive Woman prevails, and women are not perceived as simply being responsible but instead as being cold and ruthless.

Kranda (1998) indicates that today many police organizations do not have as much difficulty attracting women to the organization as they do retaining them after they have spent considerable monies on their training. She does point out, however, that organizations need to expand their recruitment efforts for women to include more institutions of higher learning instead of simply former military personnel, which tends to be primarily male. If concerted efforts are not made in areas of recruitment it is unlikely that the number of women in applicant pools will increase.

Special consideration must be given to police training programs that have the potential to make or break the recruit. Administrators must insure that the testing programs are not biased and create atmospheres that are designed to exclude women and essentially spotlight failure (Kranda, 1998). Training must support qualities that are needed in the ideal police officer, and not reflect gender-based assumptions about what the appropriate officer should be like. Instead, training should facilitate the development of officers who are able to think independently, interact well with the community, and help to resolve conflicts and provide citizens with the resources they need to improve their environment (Kranda, 1998: 54). What is considered appropriate for the contemporary police officer must adequately reflect what is needed to perform the tasks of policing in constantly changing communities, and not what has simply been described as "real police work."

The Fairfax County, Virginia, police department established a formal mentoring program in order to increase its retention rates. By incorporating a formal mentoring program into its recruitment, selection, and training programs, Fairfax County was able to increase its retention in the Academy with just one session. Prior to the institution of the formal mentoring program there were ten recruits, five of whom were women, who were lost during Academy training in the session. In the session directly following the institution of the mentoring program, only five recruits were lost following the Academy, none of whom were women (Kranda, 1998).

In another mentoring program in the Lakewood Police Department in California, a process was developed by a task force of both sworn and civilian personnel to benefit all women in the organization. By including representatives from every segment of the organization, the administration demonstrated their full commitment to the program and the valuing of all their employees (Kranda, 1998).

Formal mentoring programs must be comprehensive to be effective. What this means is that programs must involve members from their initial contact with the organization during the recruitment process, and continue at each phase of employment, from selection and hiring to training and promotion. Kranda (1998) indicates that the manner in which a new employee is transitioned into an organization can be critical to whether or not the employee remains with the organization, what opinions the employee forms of the organization, and how the employee ultimately performs (p. 56).

Although formal mentoring programs have proven to be effective in increasing retention in police organizations, it is important to note that these are not a panacea for all that plagues an organization. Mentoring programs cannot correct an ineffective applicant processing unit or enhance a training environment that focuses solely on eliminating recruits rather than developing good officers (Kranda, 1998: 56). Instead, mentoring programs must be a part of a holistic approach that includes multiple measures to address the issues faced by women in law enforcement today.

Professional Networks

Networks usually arise out of gaping holes, or places where needs are not being met (Catalyst, 1999: 2). These may be formal or informal and, according to Catalyst, are one of the best ways for women to get the career advice and support they want—and for the company to get the most out of one of its most important assets (Catalyst, 1999: 4).

Women's networks are usually established to address three problems that are common to women in the workplace:

1) The overall company environment often includes built-in assumptions that are more of a burden for women than for men. Women need to join together to bring these assumptions into the open and help the company adapt to the real requirements of modern life.
2) Company social structures tend to isolate women, making it hard for them to rely on each other for advice and support. Women need to come together to share strategies and help each other overcome this isolation.
3) Established career paths can sometimes exclude women. Women need to get together to focus on their own career development and the development of women at other levels in the organization (1999: 2–3).

Networks may employ a variety of mechanisms to address these problems, such as advising senior management, setting up mentoring programs and speaker series, and holding network events for members (Catalyst, 1999).

Professional organizations often provide excellent means for women to establish relationships with individuals within their professions. These informal relationships are useful in keeping members informed with regard to career opportunities, techniques for dealing with particular issues or problems, and influence with regard to organizational decision making.

Historically, women's organizations have been formed to provide career development. Unfortunately, women who join these types of organizations are usually the ones needing the most support from successful women, who often have limited time and resources to commit to the organizations. Moreover, some argue that women do not maximize their use of networks as effectively as men do. Often many women who join professional organizations do not attend meetings, nor do they arrange to meet with other members outside of their organizations. Those who do meet with others tend to meet with friends or internal business associates, missing the opportunity to develop new contacts or networks (DeWine and Casbolt, 1983). If women make use of professional organizations for networking, the potentials for career enhancement and development exist. In interviews of women in law enforcement today (see Chapter 9), most women indicated that they were members of at least one professional organization. Some organizations were specifically developed for women, and some organizations were for both women and men. It is possible that what appears as a lack of commitment on the part of women to attend these professional meetings or foster professional relationships outside of their organizations may be attributed to a lack of commitment of financial resources on the part of their agencies.

CONTEMPORARY RESEARCH ON MENTORING AND NETWORKING

In an effort to describe the current state of networking and mentoring in women's law enforcement, Scarborough, Collins, and Shain (2000) surveyed members of a professional women's law enforcement organization in a southeastern state. Through telephone surveys, respondents were asked questions about their attitudes toward and experiences with networking and mentoring during their law enforcement careers. This exploratory work served as a pilot study through which the survey was tested prior to a statewide survey to be administered at a later date based on the findings of the current work.

Respondents to the survey were not representative of the current total population of women in law enforcement, but nevertheless this work may serve as a starting point to guide further research. Only 6.6% of the women came from organizations with 10 or fewer sworn employees, with only 11% of the respondents coming from organizations of 20 sworn officers or fewer. Consequently, 48.9% of the respondents were from organizations with more than 100 sworn officers. This means that most of the respondents came from medium or large organizations, which would be more likely to have women officers and ones of rank that could possibly be in a better position to mentor or network. This further confirms anecdotal evidence that women who join professional organizations tend to be from larger organizations. Respondents came from different types of agencies, but the majority were from local municipal organizations.

In response to questions regarding their mentoring relationships, about one third of the women indicated that they were mentored by officers with rank (34%), and about one third indicated that they were mentored by officers with rank other than command staff (32%). Other mentors included field training officers, civilian employees, and command staff. Respondents indicated that men were more often mentors than women were. Types of mentoring, or issues about which respondents were mentored, included advancement and career development, police techniques, moral support, role modeling, and department politics, with more women indicating that they were mentoring in the area of police techniques. Women described the benefits of mentoring as falling into three broad categories: experiential similarity, personal, and professional. Experiential similarity included benefiting from hearing of their mentor's personal work experiences. Personal issues dealt with support systems, empowerment, and having a mentor as a confidence builder. Professional issues dealt with career development, recruiting, and the fact that policing is a male-dominated profession.

When asked about their networking relationships, a majority of the respondents (62%) indicated that they were not a part of any type of network, either formal or informal. Twenty percent indicated, however, that they were a part of an informal network. The remaining respondents indicated that they participated in some type of information sharing or social groups, but did not consider this networking.

Respondents were also asked questions regarding their perception of the resistance that they had encountered while working in the police organization. A majority (52%) indicated that they had not been readily accepted, while slightly less than half (41%) felt that they had been accepted. The remaining respondents indicated that they had mixed feelings about acceptance. The most common type of resistance identified by the respondents was male officers' attitudes that women should remain in more stereotypical roles, and their blatant unwillingness to work with female officers. The phrase ."women belong in the kitchen" was identified as commonly heard by several of the respondents. Other examples of resistance to women were male officers refusing to be assigned as a partner for a woman, or female officers not being called upon to provide backup for male officers.

FORMAL NETWORKING OPPORTUNITIES

Although the International Association of Women Police (IAWP) was started as the International Association of Policewomen (IAP) in 1915, it struggled organizationally until the late 1950s when it changed its name and started increasing in membership. Besides this organization, there have been no other organizations of substantial size specifically for women in law enforcement until most recently. The following organizations represent some of the organizational networking opportunities available to women in law enforcement and private security today. The International Association of Women Police, the European Network of Policewomen, the Australasian Council of Women and Policing, and the British Association of Women Police provide important formal networking opportunities, but they will be discussed in Chapter 8, "An International Perspective."

National Association of Women Law Enforcement Executives

In 1995, at the 102nd Annual Conference of the International Association of Chiefs of Police, a group of executive women from various law enforcement backgrounds established a steering committee to undertake the development of an executive women's law enforcement organization. From this steering committee, the National Association of Women Law Enforcement Executives (NAWLEE) was formed. NAWLEE is the first organization established to address the needs of women in senior management positions in law enforcement and is administered directly by current law enforcement practitioners. The organization is dedicated to serving women executives and those who have ambitions of being executives in law enforcement. The general purpose and mission of NAWLEE are to promote the ideals and principles of women executives in law enforcement; to conduct training seminars to train and educate women executives in law enforcement, including but not limited to the areas of leadership, management, and administration; to provide a forum for the exchange of information concerning law enforcement; and generally fostering effective law enforcement (NAWLEE, 1998).

National Center for Women and Policing

The National Center for Women and Policing (NCWP) is a division of the Feminist Majority Foundation, a national organization working for women's equality and empowerment, and for violence against women. The Center's mission is twofold. It is a nationwide resource for women in policing, law enforcement agencies, community leaders, and public officials seeking to increase the numbers of women in policing, and it is committed to improving the response to family violence. The Center provides training, research, education, and action programs in the following areas:

- Educational campaigns to raise awareness among decision makers and the general public about the benefits of increasing the numbers of women in policing.
- Innovative leadership training and advocacy programs to increase the numbers of women in policing and policy-making positions, including strategies to increase recruitment, hiring, and promotion of women and eliminate sexual discrimination and harassment of women officers.
- Promoting specialized Family Violence Response Protocol within law enforcement agencies for more effective police response to family violence crimes, including police family violence (NCWP, 1998).
- Providing opportunities for networking through Center-sponsored conferences to raise awareness about the aforementioned issues. The conferences target not only sworn and civilian women in policing but also national, state, and local law enforcement officials, police trainers and consultants, community leaders, public officials, academics, and educators (NCWP, 1998).

Women in Federal Law Enforcement (WIFLE)

Women in Federal Law Enforcement (WIFLE) is an organization dedicated to fostering an awareness of the significant contributions of women in federal law enforcement. WIFLE was formed through an interagency committee composed of members from the Department of the Treasury and the Department of Justice in 1982. In June 1999, WIFLE was incorporated.

Through celebrating past accomplishments, striving for new achievements, and recognizing the skills, creativity, and leadership qualities of women, WIFLE intends to improve gender equity in law enforcement. To meet these goals, WIFLE has the following objectives:

- Conduct training conferences and form a networking system.
- Conduct outreach campaigns and establish dialogues with diverse communities.
- Examine how law enforcement can better serve communities while balancing enforcement efforts.
  (http://www.ceeme.com/WIFLE)

PRIVATE SECURITY NETWORKING

Women in private security have not been as successful at establishing networks as their public law enforcement counterparts. To date there are no formalized domestic (U.S.) women security networks or organizations. Although ASIS is the largest recognized professional security organization, they have a policy of not recognizing or endorsing any special interest groups, such as for women or persons of color. However, some African American security professionals have convened meetings around the ASIS annual conference activities to challenge a number of corporations regarding their policies on hiring of minorities. Women, on the other hand, have not been able to bring a collective voice to the forefront. There are a number of professional women's business organizations, however, which may be taking the place of professional women's security organizations. There is an international organization for women in security, Women In International Security (WIIS), which was formed in 1987 as a nonprofit educational and networking organization. WIIS is dedicated to enhancing the role of women in the field of foreign and defense policy. A more detailed description of WIIS follows in Chapter 8.

Women have developed a strong economic voice in this country and appear to be using many of the same networking techniques as men, such as professional organizations. Their presence in both law enforcement and security has consistently grown and appears to have developed a foothold in what has historically been a male-dominated profession. With the success that women are having in such areas as business, law, finance, and medicine, it is only a matter of time until the phrase "male-dominated" becomes an outdated and seldom-used phrase. The success and prosperity of agencies and organizations will depend on their ability to recruit women. Peters (1999) recommends that organizations must dramatically change their recruitment efforts if they are going to attract women into their companies. He suggests that they will need to completely revamp the following:

1. Recruiting practices
2. Hiring sources
3. Promotional systems
4. Organizational structure
5. Business process
6. Vision and leadership models (Peters, 1999: 420)

Women are poised to enter this new millennium as empowered and influential players who may be viewed as making a significant and, in many cases, unique contribution to the organization. Those agencies that are successful in attracting highly qualified women into their ranks are certain to be viewed as benchmarks for others to follow.

8

An International Perspective

Research on women in policing in the United States has been described as somewhat limited. However, when compared to international research on women in policing, U.S. research is more readily available and extensive. Many reasons account for the paucity of research and information on international policewomen, including an absence of source materials, a shortage of analytical concepts and frameworks, and difficulties of cross-cultural comparisons. Specific difficulties of cross-cultural comparisons include "language problems in translations of questionnaire items; meaning equivalences of terms and concepts (is sexual harassment recognized as the same phenomenon in different cultures?); are different countries similarly experienced in research or opinion polling?" (Smith and Bond, 1993, as cited in Brown and Heidensohn, 2000: 21).

In attempts to address methodological issues with international research, researchers have used methods that are not as commonly used. For example, snowball sampling has been employed to identify small samples of survey respondents, which are highly selective. Additionally, professional organizations have served as a means through which survey respondents have been identified (Brown and Heidensohn, 2000). Although these methods provide a means through which initial base research efforts may be conducted, caution must be taken when making generalizations from this research, due to the highly selective nature of respondent identification.

The potential value of international research is unquestionable. As one researcher notes, substantial benefits may be realized from undertaking work of this kind. Bayley (1999) indicates that we can extend the knowledge of alternative possibilities, develop powerful insights into human behavior, increase the probability of reform, and gain perspectives on ourselves (Bayley, 1999, as cited in Brown and Heidensohn, 2000: 24).

Although material is limited, we have included information on European policewomen. This chapter includes an overview of the current status of international women in policing, a summary of limited research, and a review of international police organizations for women.

CURRENT STATUS OF INTERNATIONAL WOMEN POLICE

The only compilation of data on the status of international women in policing is the European Network of Policewomen (ENP) Bi-Annual report, "Facts, Figures and General Information." This report provides a general overview of the position of women within various European police forces. The first report was published in 1989, with a total of six reports having been completed.

Questions were sent to the most senior official within the policing agency in all of the participating countries of Europe. The total number of countries receiving a questionnaire was 44. The return/response to these questions has increased from 18% in 1989 to 50% in 2000. This, of course, is based upon those agencies completing and returning the questionnaire. One could not simply draw the conclusion that the increases are entirely attributable to actual increases of women in some police positions; they are due at least in part to a better return rate on the ENP questionnaire.

Tables 8.1 to 8.3 summarize the ENP data and provide a perspective on the numbers of women in policing throughout Europe. The countries have been divided by region. *Central Europe* includes Austria, Hungary, Germany, Liechtenstein, Poland, and Switzerland; *Western Europe* includes Belgium, Ireland, Luxemburg, Monaco, and The Netherlands; *Northern Europe* includes Finland, Iceland, Norway, and Sweden; *Southern Europe* includes Greece; *Southwestern Europe* includes Andorra, Portugal, and Spain; *Eastern Europe* includes Estonia, Latvia, and Lithuania; *Southwestern Asia* includes Turkey; *United Kingdom* includes England, Scotland, Wales, and Northern Ireland. These represent all of the countries that returned an ENP questionnaire.

In the European countries responding there were approximately 88,247 sworn female police officers, compared to 845,254 sworn male police officers. Women police represent about 10% of all sworn police officers in Europe.

Women in command positions vary throughout Europe, with the greatest representation in Central, Western, and Northern Europe. Table 8.2 provides a breakdown by region of the representation of policewomen in command positions.

European police departments were asked whether or not they had an Equal Opportunity Policy. Table 8.3 summarizes the results of this question.

Table 8.1   Percentage of female sworn officers by region: 1989 and 2000.

1989: % Female Officers	% Change	2000: % Female Officers
Central Europe: 2.2%	8.02%	10.22%
Western Europe: 5.15%	5.48%	10.63%
Northern Europe: 7.1%	3.29%	10.39%
Southern Europe: 8.3%	−1.35%	6.95%
Southwestern Europe: 4.5%	1.75%	6.25%
Eastern Europe: 0%	19.5%	19.5%
Average Representation of Policewomen in Europe	Total/6 Regions	10.6%

Table 8.2 Percentage of female managers in command: 2000.

Region of Europe	Regional Average
Central Europe	5.3%
Western Europe	4.1%
Northern Europe	3.1%
Southern Europe	.80%
Eastern Europe	10%
Southwestern Europe	5.2%
Southeastern Europe	.75%
Total Average of European Women Who Hold Command Positions as Compared to % in the United States	4.2%

The survey contained a question about why women leave the police service. The following represents the most common reasons in order of frequency: retirement, low salary, stress and working conditions, the work was not what they expected, career change, and failure to pass entry and/or training exams.

Pregnancy leave policies vary among the different European countries. By far, Central Europe has the most progressive policies with regard to pregnancy leave, and these countries have a specific law in place referred to as the "Maternity Protection Law." Other regions that appear to have policies in place include Northern Europe, which allows women to work part-time and to transfer or draw a pregnancy allowance. Eastern Europe permits women to have what they refer to as "Temporary Easement of Conditions of Service and Transfer to Another Position." They also specify that "pregnant women may not be employed on duty, outside working hours, during the night, on holidays or on festive days. It is also forbidden to decrease a woman's salary due to her pregnancy or to dismiss her." Of all of the regions throughout Europe, Western Europe has the fewest pregnancy leave policies and also prohibits pregnant women from "working in the streets."

Table 8.3   Equal opportunity policies for European regions.

European Region	Number of Agencies with an Equal Opportunity Employer	Number of Agencies with a Sexual Harassment Policy	Number of Agencies That Do Not Have an Equal Opportunity Policy	Number of Agencies That Do Not Have a Sexual Harassment Policy
Southwestern Europe	2	0	1	3
Central Europe	16 (1993 Law of Equal Treatment)	11	5	10
Eastern Europe	2	1	3	4
Western Europe	2	3	3	2
Northern Europe	3	3	1	1
Southern Europe	0	0	1	1
Southeastern Europe	1	1	0	0
Southwestern Asia	0	0	1	1
United Kingdom	2	2	0	0

Although the ENP survey is limited by its reliance on a single mailing to a "high ranking" law enforcement official, it serves as one of the only comprehensive international assessments of the current status of women in policing. Much can be learned from the data gathered from the survey, but caution should be taken in trying to generalize about the current status of international women in policing. The survey should be used as a general overview of women in law enforcement and serve to provide a starting point for further research and evaluation.

RESEARCH

Previous cross-cultural research on women in policing is scant, with Heidensohn (1992), Brown (1997), and Brown and Heidensohn (2000) appearing to have the most comprehensive works. Brown and Heidensohn's (2000) most recent work includes a theoretical framework to examine women in policing, a historical analysis of the evolution of women in policing, original empirical research using both discourse analysis and survey research, and a summary of the international works of others. We give specific attention to this work, for it is not only the most recent but also one that provides a thorough assessment of the other works to date.

Brown and Heidensohn's (2000) work focuses on three specific elements: structural relations, conceptual content, and cross-cultural comparison (p. 4). Structural relations include time and numbers. Noting arguments both for and against retrospective studies, the authors "sought to salvage past practices and culture within police organizations in order to obtain some purchase on present attitudes towards women police officers that contribute to the continued presence of discriminatory behavior" (2000: 5). In describing women in this retrospective analysis, Brown and Heidensohn (2000) classify them into three categories: the early 1900s to World War II (elders), post–World War II to the 1960s (seasoned), and the 1970s to the present (fledgling). When examining numbers, they draw heavily on the work of Kanter (previously discussed in Chapter 1), who contends that women are often viewed as "tokens" in the workplace, depending on their representation (1977).

Brown and Heidensohn (2000) surveyed 804 women in 35 countries with the help of the research departments of the Garda Siochana and Royal Ulster Constabulary, the British Association of Women Police, the ENP, the International Association of Women Police (IAWP), Australasian policewomen, and women in the African police forces of Malawi and Botswana. Women in this sample indicated that they are most frequently "white, 'thirty-something,' have served an average of 12 years, are likely to be married or living with a partner, have no children, and work as a patrol officer or a detective" (Brown and Heidensohn, 2000: 109).

The researchers were particularly interested in the following areas: discrimination, coping and support strategies, self-efficacy as related to police culture, and the validity of their proposed taxonomy of police organizations. Responses indicated that 20% were unaccepted by at least some of their male colleagues, with over 75% having experienced some type of sexual harassment from a male colleague. Only 5% of the respondents felt unaccepted by their female colleagues. The most frequently cited form of sex discrimination against these women was differential deployment.

Brown and Heidensohn (2000) found that women police use a variety of coping strategies to combat challenges in the police organization. A majority (51%) of respondents indicated that they used assertiveness as a means with which to cope, while slightly under half (45%) of the respondents used joking as another means of dealing with adverse situations. Most used support strategies, including gaining extra skills (66%), working harder (65%), and using senior male officers. Additionally, no matter how long policewomen had served in organizations, it appeared that their level of acceptance by other police officers was similar, as previously indicated.

Brown and Heidensohn's (2000) work has set the stage for international research on women and policing by not only providing a theoretical framework with which to pursue these efforts, but also an offer of practical implications that could readily impact the organizations' receptivity to women. Through the lenses provided by these authors, the organizations can be seen with clarity with the hope of making the environments friendlier for women.

INTERNATIONAL LAW ENFORCEMENT ORGANIZATIONS FOR WOMEN

There are four major international private and public law enforcement organizations for women. They are the Women In International Security (WIIS), the International Association of Women Police

(IAWP), the European Network of Policewomen (ENP), and the Australasian Council of Women and Police. The ENP also has numerous affiliate organizations throughout Europe.

Women In International Security (WIIS)

As discussed in Chapter 7, the Women In International Security (WIIS) organization was formed in 1987 as a nonprofit educational and networking organization. The membership of WIIS is made up of women and men from academia, think tanks, the diplomatic corps, the intelligence community, the military, and the private sector. Currently there are approximately 1,000 members, with 450 from the United States, 113 international members, 280 student members, and 60 male members.

WIIS and its members are involved in issues impacting international security, ranging from arms control, arms transfers in the Third World, and ethnic conflict resolution to democratization in Latin America, and the development of international trade blocs. The organization focuses on the following:

(1) Maintaining a computerized databank of women in the field of international security.

(2) Organizing a seminar series and conferences highlighting women speakers on current issues.

(3) Distributing professional information in directories such as *Internships in Foreign and Defense Policy: A Complete Guide for Women (and Men)* and *Fellowships in International Affairs: A Guide to Opportunities in the United States and Abroad.*

(4) Sponsoring the Summer Symposium for graduate students in international affairs.

(5) Sponsoring a Post-Doctoral Fellowship in Security Studies at the Center for International and Security Studies at Maryland.

(6) Serving as a clearinghouse for information for and about women in foreign and defense policy.

(7) Maintaining an international network with women working on international issues in Russia, the NIS, Eastern and Western Europe, Asia, and elsewhere around the globe.

WIIS maintains a computerized directory of women working in the field of international security, which allows for the identification of women based upon their professional background and areas of expertise. As of this publication this was the only professional security organization identified for women.

International Association of Women Police (IAWP)

The IAWP is the oldest of the organizations specifically dedicated to promoting women in law enforcement. First organized as the International Association of Policewomen (IAP) in 1915, it was chartered in 1916, in Washington, D.C. In 1932, after some years of struggle, the IAP temporarily disbanded before some of it programs and ideals had been brought to fruition. In 1956, in San Diego, California, at a meeting of the San Diego Women Peace Officers of California, the association was reorganized as the International Association of Women Police. The following year at Purdue University, the first biannual meeting of IAWP was held. As the newly elected President, Dr. Lois Higgins, a 30-year veteran of the Chicago Police Department, directed the growth and activities of the organization for eight years. She then served IAWP as Executive Director for the following 12 years. Significant accomplishments of IAWP during its development include the promotion of separate women's bureaus for women officers, the development of the *IAWP Bulletin*, which has been replaced by *Women Police*, the organization's official publication, and the establishment of annual training conferences.

The vision of the IAWP is "a world where women working in the criminal justice professions are treated justly, fairly, and equitably by the agencies they serve" (IAWP, 2001). Consequently, to achieve this vision, the mission of IAWP is to "insure equity for women in the criminal justice field . . . [to] strive to achieve this mission by utilizing, investing, and celebrating the individual strengths, talents, and skills of our members" (IAWP, 2001).

In order to achieve this vision, the IAWP has the following goals:

 ♦ Act as a strong, interrelated network and support system
 ♦ Provide training and network opportunities

+ Serve as a comprehensive source of information and referral
+ Provide professional and technical expertise
+ Require organizational and individual ethical behavior and accountability
+ Increase awareness
+ Encourage women to enter the criminal justice field (IAWP, 1999)

European Network of Policewomen (ENP)

The ENP is an official Non-Governmental Organization (NGO) in consultative status to the United Nations. It consists of a foundation with an international board of 26 formal members, represented by 18 European countries. The primary focus of this organization is to improve the position of police women within European police forces. ENP organizes conferences, projects, and seminars independently or in cooperation with some of the following agencies:

+ Dutch Police Selection and Training Institute (LSOP)
+ Polizei Fuhrungs Akademie in Munster, Germany, in the development of a German Career Development training course
+ Association of European Police Colleges
+ European Law Enforcement Coordination (ELEC)

The ENP was founded at the International Conference for Policewomen held in Noordwijkerhout, The Netherlands, on March 23, 1989. They have successfully organized and sponsored nearly two dozen conferences and workshops over the last decade. The ENP has directed their organizational activities in the following areas:

Conferences and Seminars:
+ Sexual Harassment within the European Police
+ Equal Opportunities for Women
+ Women in European Policing
+ Combating Violence Against Women
+ Career Development Seminars for Policewomen

- Policing in East-European Democracies
- International Police Training Course
- Female Police Managers
- European Networking Conference

Training and Research:
- Publication of "Facts, Figures and General Information," which is in its fifth edition
- Study on "Equal Treatment of Policewomen in the European Community"
- Publication on "Equal Pay/Equal Treatment amongst Policewomen"
- Publication on "Violence against Women and the Role of the Police"
- Network training for the Polish Centre for promotion of policewomen
- Publication of "Women in European Policing, What's It All About?"

Networks/Country Activities:
- Established the ENP in Germany, 1993
- Established the Hungarian Association of Policewomen, 1993
- Established the Association of Belgian Policewomen, 1994
- Established the Centre of Promotion of Women in the Polish Police, 1996
- Established the ENP in Bulgaria, 1997

Public Relations and Marketing:
- Video production of a film: "Everything you always wanted to know about policewomen"
- ENP delegation to the fourth United Nations conference on Women in Beijing, China
- Introduction of a number of policy plans regarding women in policing

The ENP has contributed significantly to the body of literature on topics related to women in policing and violence against women.

Since 1991 they have published nearly a dozen reports on these two topics alone. Currently, the ENP has national chapters in the following countries: Austria, Belgium, Bulgaria, Finland, Germany, Hungary, Iceland, The Netherlands, Poland, Slovak Republic, Sweden, and the United Kingdom.

Australasian Council of Women and Policing

The Australasian Council of Women and Policing is a professional association that focuses on representing women in policing at a broader government level such as the educational, industrial, and professional sectors. It was officially formed in 1997. Its articulated purposes are to:

- Create an Australasian link in the global networking of women in policing;
- Improve the position of women within policing;
- Improve the relationship between policing and women in the community.

The Council has set as its goals the development of an Australasian information exchange network with women in policing throughout Australia and Asia as well as establishing policing networks in other countries. They plan on having biannual conferences on women and policing, developing an independent resource center for women and policing, and providing independent advisors to community groups and committees. They have also published the *Journal of Australasian Council of Women and Policing*, with the first issue appearing in December of 1998.

Although information on women in policing internationally is limited, the research base that has been started certainly offers a framework with which to continue efforts that can only be fruitful. By promoting communication and collaboration through professional organizations bound together by common interests, improvements for policewomen abroad will continue and consequently serve to make the profession of policing one of quality that serves all citizens equally.

9

Women Speak Out

Much of the research on women in law enforcement has omitted their subjective experiences, and instead has focused on others' perceptions of them. Fletcher (1995), however, captured some of their experiences in her recent qualitative work interviewing contemporary women law enforcement officers about various subjects such as training, the code of silence, home life, and the uniform. Gossett and Williams (1998) interviewed women officers regarding their perceptions of discrimination. Neither of these works was intended to be generalizable, but instead attempted to give women a voice, with a snapshot of their thoughts and feelings at a given point in time. Following that model, this chapter presents interviews of women in law enforcement today, with no attempt at generalizability, but offering the rich insight that only qualitative research can yield.

METHODOLOGY

Phone interviews were conducted during Fall 1998 and Spring 1999 using membership lists of professional law enforcement organizations for women. Snowball sampling was used to identify additional women who might be interviewed for this work. A total of 46 women from both law enforcement and private security were interviewed.

Table 9.1   Demographic characteristics of the sample.

Age	Race	College	Salary
35–44 (N = 21) 46%	White (N = 44) 96%	No College Degree (N = 14) 30%	$25,000–$45,000 (N = 6) 13%
45–54 (N = 20) 43%	African American (N = 1) 2%	2-Year Degree (N = 3) 7%	$46,000–$64,000 (N = 17) 37%
55–64 (N = 4) 9%	Hispanic (N = 1) 2%	4-Year Degree (N = 13) 28%	$65,000+ (N = 21) 46%
65+ (N = 1) 2%		Master's of Science Degree (N = 13) 28%	Unknown (N = 2) 4%
		Terminal Degree Ph.D. (N = 1) <1% Ed.D. (N = 1) <1% J.D. (N = 1) 7%	

Questions included demographics, as well as a series of open-ended questions, asking women to comment on their perceptions of issues such as barriers they have faced and mentoring. A summary of the demographics is presented (see Table 9.1), as well as excerpts from the open-ended questions that represent majority viewpoints or provide particularly salient comments.

DEMOGRAPHIC CHARACTERISTICS OF RESPONDENTS

Although a wide range of occupations are covered, some of the demographic characteristics of the respondents are very similar. Forty-six women responded to the survey, with 36 representing police and 10 representing private security. The women ranged in age from 35 to 65 and over, with almost half indicating that they were 35–44 (N = 21) and half indicating that they were 45–54 (N = 20). Ninety-six percent (N = 44) of the respondents were white, with two African-American women and one Hispanic woman responding.

Seventy percent of the women had some type of college degree (N = 30), with over half of the women having a four-year degree or higher (N = 29). Thirty percent (N = 14), however, had no degree at all. The range of income for the respondents was $25,000 to greater than $65,000. Forty-six percent (N = 21) of the women indicated that they made over $65,000, while 37% (N = 17) indicated that they made between $46,000 and $64,000. A mere 13% (N = 6) of the respondents indicated that they made between $25,000 and $45,000.

A variety of organizations were represented by the respondents and include federal law enforcement agencies; state police agencies; large, medium, and small city and rural police departments; sheriff's departments; campus police/security organizations; security equipment companies; contract security companies; industrial security; office building security; law enforcement academies; telecommunications security; security consultants; and security software companies. Respondents represented all regions of the country. One-third (N = 15) of the women worked in the southern states, with almost one-fourth (N = 10) in the Midwest. The mid-Atlantic, southwest, and Pacific coast states each had 11% (N = 5) of the respondents, while the northeast and Rocky Mountains states had less than 10% each (N = 3 and N = 2, respectively).

Three of the open-ended questions were evaluated and are presented below. The questions are: (1) What do you feel is your greatest barrier/obstacle in your field? (2) Over the course of time, what has been the most significant change that has taken place in your profession? and (3) Describe any mentors, specifying male or female, that have helped you in your career.

GREATEST BARRIER/OBSTACLE IN YOUR FIELD

The majority of the women interviewed indicated that they had faced some type of barrier or another over the course of their professional careers. Those barriers fall into one of the following categories: "good old boys" network and negative attitudes toward women; balancing family and work; politics and bureaucracy; gender; age; and financial restraints of the organization. Some of the women (13%) indicated that they had not faced any barriers in their professional career. Additional barriers that were identified but found with less frequency include knowledge and training, situational obstacles, and acceptance of their expertise in their field.

Good Old Boys Network and Negative Attitudes toward Women (30%)

Thirty percent of the women indicated that the "good old boys" network and negative attitudes toward women in these types of professions were the greatest barriers or obstacles in their current positions. Most of the women did not elaborate, but made comments such as, "*Unfortunately, I think there are still some of the good ole boy networks in law enforcement in general. The greatest barrier is that it is a male-dominated career, however, I do not make it or let it be an obstacle . . .*" The following comments were made by a woman working in the sale of security equipment and technology:

The ol' boy network. It's hard for women in my work to break through that barrier that men place on the jobs our business does. They often perceive women as not being knowledgeable enough to take care of and run the equipment we use because a lot of it is very high tech.

A supervisor of investigations in a large metropolitan police department had this to say about barriers: "*Not faced many barriers based on my gender, although still a white male-based hierarchy for the most part.*" An Assistant Chief of a large southern metropolitan police department also stated that "*some attitudes by the old boy network*" were one of the barriers she faced in her position. A civilian working as a Director of Administration in a southwest police department stated that a significant barrier is, "*gaining acceptance as a law enforcement professional from the sworn officers that I work with. It's improving here, but there is a great need for equal respect and equal pay for the work I do.*" A Captain of a large southwest metropolitan police department indicated that "*there are still some men that feel women can't fill some positions."* A Deputy Chief in a Midwest police department was quoted as saying *"dealing with male officers who don't like working for females"* had been her greatest barrier.

Others indicated that although the good old boys had been a problem early on in their careers, that was not necessarily the case now. According to an Assistant Police Chief in Wisconsin, *"Well, I don't think we have so much of this in our department, but I would have to say that the leftover attitudes, the outdated attitudes of people, are the greatest barrier. We have a lot of positions held by women: the chief of police at the local University is a woman; the Mayor is a woman; and we have two women serving on the* [state] *Supreme Court, to mention a few."*

Balancing Family and Work (13%)

The issue of trying to balance family and work was cited by 13% of the women interviewed as a significant issue. According to a supervisor in the investigations unit of a large metropolitan police department in Texas, *"There is an innate discrimination based on women being the main caretakers of our children in this society. I was often forced to choose between work and home. Most men never took that into consideration when making their decision[s] because they had a wife at home taking care of their children."* An FBI agent, located in a large northeastern city, comments that *"family commitments are of greater consideration for the female agents than for the male agents."* A Captain with a Florida Sheriff's Department simply stated that it was *"difficult balancing home life and work."* A Captain with a California police department described her problem of balancing family and work in one word, her *"husband."* A sergeant with a large police department in southern Florida felt that her greatest barrier was balancing *"family and shift work."*

No Barriers (13%)

A former Captain with a medium-sized metropolitan police department remarked that she was *"delighted that I don't feel there were any barriers. There was the occasional male/female thing, I guess, but within my peer group at the department I don't feel like I had any.*"

A factory representative for a security access systems company indicated that "*I don't feel I have barriers I cannot overcome.*"

Politics and Bureaucracy (11%)

This was listed as a barrier by 5 of the 46 women interviewed. Most of the women identifying this as a barrier did not provide any details other than to say that the presence of politics or the bureaucracy associated with many of police departments posed the greatest stumbling block for their advancement into a Chief's position. A U.S. Customs Agent was quoted as saying the greatest barrier was "*politics; Customs is under a microscope at this point.*" A unit commander for a Michigan police department indicated that her biggest barrier was "*the bureaucracy of the department.*"

Financial Restraints of the Organization (11%)

Limited resources and the size of the organization was identified as a barrier by 5 of the 46 women interviewed. They saw this as being their greatest barrier to equal pay and promotional opportunities. A security manager of a building complex in Chicago stated that "*there is mostly a money factor of who's getting paid how much. I'm sure that there are many men in the same position as me or* [who] *make more money than I do.*" A state police Bureau Chief felt that "*financial resources as well as head count*" were significant barriers in her organization. The Chief of Police in a suburb of Illinois indicated that "*the budget*" was her greatest obstacle in running the police department.

Gender (11%)

An equal number of women responded to gender as an obstacle or barrier as did to balancing family and work and to financial restraints of the organization. Although their comments were often simply the fact that being a woman was a barrier, a patrol sergeant from a

Colorado Police Department stated, "*My size caused the greatest barrier.*" Evidently, because of her gender and relatively small size, she faced barriers in her organization. In another example, a sergeant in a small to medium town in Illinois suggested that her department was "*behind in gender and diversity issues.*"

Age (4%)

Only two of the women interviewed indicated that their age was a barrier for them in their current positions. One of the two women who felt that their age was a factor stated that "*there has been so many different obstacles over the years, but right now I would have to say my age.*" She is currently a Captain in a Midwestern law enforcement academy where she teaches juvenile law, child abuse, and firearms instruction. The other woman who indicated that age is a barrier was an investigator with a college campus security department in the state of New York. She felt that age was more of a barrier for her now than it had been previously. It is interesting that these women found their age to be a barrier, since both were in the 35 to 54 age group, which is still considered young by today's standards.

CAREER CHOICE

The following excerpts were taken from the survey and provide an interesting look at why women have chosen either public law enforcement or private security as a career. Their reasons for choosing these professions vary tremendously. The first category of responses includes those which indicate that these women were not actually seeking careers like this, they just "happened upon them."

"I got a clearance for a company I was working for and they said we don't have a security manager so you're it. I didn't really choose security, it just happened."

"I didn't choose security, it chose me. I was managing the [security] group and it just fell onto me."

"I was interested in college, but didn't pursue it. I just kind of fell into it."

"I didn't choose it, I just fell onto it."

"I didn't really choose it, it just kind of evolved—I just fell onto it."

"I didn't necessarily choose it. I needed a job."

"Been doing this for 21 years. Wanted to try—didn't go to school for this."

"Well, law enforcement started as an elective for me—I wanted to do research, really, and then I just kind of fell into it."

The next group of women chose their profession because of the challenge, excitement, or certain occupational characteristics of law enforcement.

"Well, it's been so long I think I've forgotten. There were lots of reasons. One reason was I was interested in it. Law enforcement offered a variety of challenges, and at that time it was almost unheard of for women to take part in law enforcement careers. I think it was maybe because someone told me I couldn't."

"Sounded like a job that was interesting and I like being my own boss."

"Well, actually, I work in the administration part of it; I'm not a sworn officer. I chose to be an administrative analyst and the opening just happened to be at the police department. But what has kept me here has been the challenge and the satisfaction that I receive from seeing the positive results in the community that are the outcome of my behind-the-scenes work."

"I chose it for the adrenaline aspect—I know that sounds weird, but it's the truth."

"It just kind of evolved. I'm an artist and I enjoy the formation of things. It evolved somewhat from working with handwriting—not really a choice I guess. I got started in it, and now I'm just rolling along."

"I chose it because of the diversity of responsibilities that it has, the traveling that it allows, the opportunity to meet so many new people, and the financial independence that it provides me."

"I chose law enforcement because it is a challenging job and the benefits are good."

"I found this particular field—forensics—very interesting. It demands a level of independent thinking that I find ideal."

"Challenging—not preplanned."

"Because of my love of investigation work."

"Action oriented; challenging (intellectually and physically); serves the public. I view it as a high calling. I work with very special people with a common purpose: protect people, prevent crime, problem solve, and go where no one else would dare to."

Some women indicated that they either had always wanted to do the job, or they had been influenced as a young person, either by a family member or role model, to pursue a career in law enforcement.

"A high school law class was really interesting, and the teacher helped me out a great deal in getting me interested. I've really just always been interested in law enforcement/security."

"Teenage decision; law enforcement female at the time; publicity."

"I wanted to be a police officer since I was 9 years old."

"I always wanted to."

"My father is in it. This was not my first choice, nursing was."

"I always wanted to be in law enforcement."

"I was interested from teen years on."

It is not uncommon to hear individuals indicate that they chose a law enforcement profession because they wanted to "help" people and be a part of the community. That same desire is apparent in some of these respondents.

"Changing circumstances in law enforcement and helping people."

"Did it for community."

"I chose law enforcement because I like helping people."

"I originally wanted to go into federal foreign service. After year 8 with metropolitan police department, I felt comfortable as a police officer. I get satisfaction from helping people."

"To make a difference; to have variety; to reach the top."

"The sense of accomplishment of offering assistance to others."

A final group of individuals indicated that they wanted to join law enforcement for numerous reasons and ones not necessarily related to characteristics of the job, but that were more likely to include motivating factors such as money or education.

"I chose it for the opportunity. Also, I was the first female to work for the Indiana International Airport Police, which was quite a challenge."

"I chose law enforcement because in 1972 it gave me a man's salary and great benefits."

"Paid better than traditional female jobs, and I got to work outside instead of being stuck inside. As the years went on, it still paid better, plus it was a lot of fun, a challenge, and I liked it. Can't think of any job over that past years that I would have rather done."

"Money: I was teaching at a Junior College and was a single parent at the time. It was right after legislation in '73 highlighted crime control and civil rights. It was a big opening for women, and I took advantage of it— at that time it paid $4,000 more than teaching. I wanted the money."

"I began in 1974, opportunity for equal pay for the job."

"Job security and benefits."

"Well, first of all, one reason is that when I started working here there weren't any women in the department. But I guess my desire was initially lit when I was a junior in college at Kent State and the National Guard came in and killed several students. I've always wanted to understand the way people's minds work, and that incident really sparked my drive to figure out and better understand the system of law enforcement, because I wanted to know what could cause the law to act in the way that it did when it took the lives of several college students."

"I had 3 years of college, then I applied because of interest in criminal justice. I come from a legal family."

As indicated, a number of the respondents stated that they did not necessarily set out to pursue a profession in law enforcement or private security. That is, it "just happened" or they "fell into it." Others clearly set their sites on a career in law enforcement. One respondent stated that she knew she wanted to be a police officer when she was 9 years old. Some women became interested in the profession based upon a course that they had taken in college. For those entering the profession in the 1970s, money was a motivator for selecting this profession. At that time law enforcement positions were paying more than the traditional female jobs.

MOST SIGNIFICANT CHANGE IN YOUR PROFESSION

The respondents were asked to describe, over the course of time, what had been the single most important event that had occurred in their career field. The following illustrates, based upon the perceptions of the interviewee, these changes. The first group of women indicated that the most significant change that took place was a change in not only the number of women and people of color in the organization but also the appearance of the office in general.

"Seeing more women in the field."

"The labor market has tightened; unemployment in our area is now 1.7%."

"When I first began my career there were no women in patrol at my department. Women didn't even receive the same training as men, and, at that time, when a woman was hired it was like she was put under a microscope. However, now it's not like that in my department. Women are considered part of the team. I give credit partially to the fact that my department is a very educated force."

"The biggest change was when I was promoted to Sergeant."

"The look of the office has changed. It is much more diverse. When I first started the office was composed primarily of white males. But now, there are more women—not a whole lot, but definitely more. Also, we have a representative of almost every ethnic background you could think of working in our offices—not a lot of each, but certainly a variety."

"The most significant change is that my police department has gone from having very few women in the rank of police officer to having the highest percentage of women police officers in the country. We've made major strides with respect to that aspect of change. The strides that women in policing have taken would have to be the most significant change."

Another group of women indicated that the most significant change was a change in the organizational philosophy, which could have resulted in the way their jobs were done, or structured.

"Introduction of the Community Policy Philosophy."

"The merging of companies."

"The most significant change would have to be the cooperation among task forces such as the FBI, ATF, and Marshals working together, as well as state and local organizations. For the longest time there have been conflicts between groups that has caused some real hassles. However, now things are much better between our task force and the others mentioned."

"The 'civilianization' of law enforcement and the emerging respect for non-sworn officers who work in law enforcement."

"The fact that a police department actually has a special unit for domestic violence victims."

"The professionalism has definitely changed. The level of education has also greatly increased."

"The educational aspect has changed the most—people involved in law enforcement are more educated now. Degrees such as Master's, Ph.D.s, and even four-year degrees are becoming expected and sought. I think that because of the increase in education that law enforcement officials are obtaining, the professionalism of the field is definitely being enhanced."

"Sexual harassment became a coined term. Family violence became a recognized problem. Women in patrol became commonplace."

"The most significant change has been the government returning control to the contractors. Which basically has to do with the government empowering the contractors to do things they should have already done."

"Security has become so mainstream. The awareness of security has really increased."

"People are realizing the need for security everywhere, not just in urban areas."

"How the police department is starting to get back in touch with the community and is allowing the community to be more involved."

Finally, some women indicated that the advent of technology has caused significant changes in their fields, which can greatly contribute to how the work is done, or what kind of people are needed to do the work.

"DNA: Prior to DNA Technology, coming into forensic science, it was difficult to identify who a biological stain came from. Now, though, it is becoming so precise that we're almost to the point of pinpointing a person's identity."

"The acceptance of women and minorities and the increase in technology."

"People do not write as much as they used to. With the increase in technology (computer, fax, instant communication sources) detecting fraud has definitely changed a bit."

"The acceptance of women—being the first woman to ever work for an organization really has proven just how much things have changed and are changing."

"Better technology in both surveillance and X-ray machines would have to be the most significant change in the security technology industry."

A common theme that appeared throughout the responses to this question was the increase in the number of women entering these predominantly male professions, and that for nearly a quarter of a century the presence of women in law enforcement and private security has steadily increased over time. Many of the women with more than 20 years' experience can look around and see that they are no longer alone. In essence, their efforts have paved the way for more women to enter these professions.

IMPACT OF MENTORS

The women surveyed were asked to describe whether or not they had any mentors, male or female, that helped them in their careers. The majority of respondents indicated that they had in fact had mentors throughout their career and that the mentors had been helpful to them professionally. Most women indicated that they had only men, or both women and men as mentors. The following describes some of those who had only female mentors:

"A former female superior really helped guide me."

"A female attorney, women officers who came before me, and the International Association of Women Police members—they've all provided me with support, guidance, and confidence through the years."

Many women had only male mentors during their careers. Obviously, this is in part due to the limited numbers of women in the profession.

"My current boss, who is male, has been a great example for me and is someone that I hope to be like in my career."

"Male, provided encouragement."

"The director of firearms instruction. When he passed away I took over his position."

"My former chief. He provided me with opportunities and encouraged me to go to training. He provided the incentives and opportunities."

"Male district and branch managers."

"Yes, male—I know that's the wrong answer, but it's the truth. He really helped me by introducing me to the right people. He has given me a lot of contacts."

"Two people, who were both male. One worked in inspections and the other worked in head security for a neighboring county. They were helpful to me with questions and answers. They allowed me to bounce questions off of them—they were kind of a resource or reference for me. I'll tell you who really helps me—my own guards; I'm tough on them, but they are very responsive and helpful."

"I had a male mentor who allowed me to make decisions, was loyal to me, and provided growth opportunities for me."

"Former male supervisor was supportive, sensitive, encouraged me, good role model, when there were no females to lead the way."

"The assistant chief. He gave me a lot of special assignments—he really believed in diversity. Also, my husband, who is a retired assistant chief. I learned a lot of lessons just by watching him. He's been very supportive throughout my career."

"My husband, who is also in law enforcement. I have benefited from his strong leadership."

"Partners who set a good example and encouraged me. No formal system. Hardly any females on the department when I started and none were mentors. Probably more outside the department have been mentors than inside. My husband and my friends have been a great support."

"I had two college professors who were both male that I would have considered to be tutors rather than mentors. They were both willing to help me out beyond the classroom."

"I've not had any formal mentors, however, I've had both male and female supervisors along the way who have acted as mentors by trying to help me in my career path."

"A male who taught me about the business world: how to dress, how to act in public, etc."

"I had a male boss once who expected me to reach my goals and the goals he set forth for me. Once I reached those goals, he would expect even more from me. He really helped me grow and develop."

Some women had both male and female mentors. Quite obviously, mentors had significant impacts on them, regardless of their gender.

"Well, I have had quite a few. A female instructor in document examining; two men who are both deceased. They were all experts in the field and very knowledgeable people."

"Primary mentors have been male, but some senior females in the organization and my current lieutenant who is female."

"All of my mentors have been male with one exception. They were fair, experienced, and open-minded."

"I have had both male and female mentors. The female ones have helped me learn persistence and tenacity. The male ones have been of more help with the mechanics of my jobs as I've moved up through the ranks; they've helped me to learn my way through jobs and projects."

"I had one female mentor who always tried to inform the female recruits to take care of themselves."

"I have experienced numerous mentors over the length of my career, both male and female. There was one male agent who ultimately got me where I am today, though, and it's because of him that I've gotten where I am today."

"I've had numerous [mentors]. There was one accountant who worked for a company in which I did who was male. He saw my potential and took me under his wing and challenged my abilities. Also, the female who held my position before me was a role model to me. She included me in decision-making events and treated me fairly. She always tried to stretch my abilities and challenge me to go beyond what I thought I was capable of. There is also another male, my current chief of police, who has provided many opportunities along my career path."

"I've had both male and female mentors. The male mentor I had was the director of security, and I learned an awful lot from him. He was an extremely thorough man, academically speaking. The female mentor provided mostly general guidance and management style. She acknowledged that I had the potential for growth and allowed me to grow—and from what I hear it's a big deal to have a woman superior see [your] potential for growth and allow [you] to grow."

"Three separate males in different areas of law enforcement that always encouraged me and treated me with respect."

The most interesting fact regarding mentors is that the majority did have mentors and, for the most part, they were males. These male colleagues and supervisors had a tremendously positive impact on the women surveyed. They credited these male mentors with their success and enthusiasm as law enforcement and private security professionals.

This research was intended to give women in contemporary law enforcement, policing, and private security a voice to provide insight into what the work world of today is like, as compared to that in years gone by. It is evident that changes have occurred in these fields since women began making significant strides in the 1960s and 1970s. It is also apparent from these interviews that some of the same barriers and problematic issues still plague women in these male-dominated organizations. Through exploratory research like this, the picture should become clearer to us and give us guidance as to how to address some of these old yet still problematic issues. By continuing to examine women in law enforcement, it is possible to identify and develop new and creative means for not only creating equal opportunities for women, but also, we hope, to make law enforcement organizations more satisfying places to work for all employees.

References List

Alex, N. *Black in Blue: A Study of the Negro Policeman*. New York: Appleton-Century-Crofts. 1969.

Ayoob, M.F. "Perspectives on Female Troopers." *Trooper*. 3. 1978. pp. 99–101, 103.

Balkin, J. "Why Policemen Don't Like Policewomen." *Journal of Police Science and Administration*. 16 (1). 1988. pp. 29–38.

Bartell Associates. *The Study of Police Women Competency in the Performance of Sector Police Work in the City of Philadelphia*. State College, PA: Author. 1978.

Bartlett, H.W., and A. Rosenblum. *Policewoman Effectiveness*. Denver, CO: Civil Service Commission and Denver Police Department. 1977.

Bartol, C.R., G.T. Bergen, J.S. Volckens, and K.M. Knoras. "Women in Small-Town Policing: Job Performance and Stress." *Criminal Justice and Behavior*. 19 (3). Sept. 1992. pp. 240–259.

Bayley, D.H. "Policing the World Stage." In Mawby, R. (ed.), *Policing Across the World*. London: UCL Press. 1999.

Baynard, V.L., and S.A. Graham-Beermann. "Can Women Cope? A Gender Analysis of Theories of Coping with Stress." *Psychology of Women Quarterly*. 17. 1993. pp. 303–318.

Belknap, J. "Women in Conflict: An Analysis of Women Correctional Officers." *Women & Criminal Justice*. 2. 1991. pp. 89–116.

Belknap, J., and J.K. Shelley. "The New Lone Ranger: Policewomen on Patrol." *American Journal of Police*. 12. 1992. pp. 47–75.

Bell, D.J. "Policewomen: Myths and Reality." *Journal of Police Science and Administration*. 10. 1982. pp. 112–120.

Bloch, P., and D. Anderson. *Policewomen on Patrol: Final Report*. Washington, DC: Urban Institute. 1974.

Brown, J. "Women in Policing: A Comparative Research Perspective." *International Journal of the Sociology of the Law*. 25. 1997. pp. 1–19.

Brown, J., and F. Heidensohn. *Gender and Policing: Comparative Perspectives*. New York: St. Martin's Press. 2000.

Buzawa, E.S. "Determining Patrol Officer Job Satisfaction: The Role of Selected Demographic and Job-Specific Attitudes." *Criminology*. 22. 1984. pp. 61–81.

Buzawa, E., T. Austin, and J. Bannon. "The Role of Selected Socio-Demographic and Job-Specific Variables in Predicting Patrol Officer Job Satisfaction: A Reexamination Ten Years Later." *American Journal of Police*. 13. 1994. pp. 51–75.

California Highway Patrol. *Women Traffic Officer Report: Final Report*. Sacramento, CA: Author. 1976.

Callan, J.M. *Women in Security Management: A Status Report*. Arlington, VA: American Society for Industrial Security. 1995.

Catalyst. *Advancing Women in Business: The Catalyst Guide*. San Francisco: Jossey-Bass Publications. 1998.

Catalyst. *Creating Women's Networks: A Catalyst Guide*. San Francisco: Jossey-Bass. 1999.

Charles, M.T. "The Performance and Socialization of Female Recruits in the Michigan State Police Training Academy." *Journal of Police Science and Administration*. 9. 1981. pp. 209–223.

Charles, M.T., and K. Parsons. "Female Performance in the Law Enforcement Function: A Review of Past Research, Current Issues and Future Potential." *Law and Order*. 26 (1). 1978. pp. 18–74.

Christophe, M. "Androgynous Management." *Women Police*. 22. 1988. pp. 6–7.

Cleaver, J. "Global Pathbreakers: Avon." *Working Woman*. January 2000. pp. 50–56.

Collins, P.A., T.A. Ricks, and C.W. Van Meter. *Principles of Security and Crime Prevention, Fourth Edition*. Cincinnati, OH: Anderson Publishing Co. 2000.

Collins, P.H. *Black Feminist Thought: Knowledge, Consciousness, and the Politics of Empowerment*. New York: Routledge, Chapman and Hall. 1991.

Couper, D.C., and Lobitz, S.H. "Quality Leadership: The First Step Towards Quality Policing." *Police Chief*. 55 (4). 1988. pp. 79–84.

Cunningham, W.C., J.J. Strauchs, and C.W. Van Meter. *Private Security Trends: 1970 to 2000, The Hallcrest Report II*. Stoneham, MA: Hallcrest Systems. 1990.

Daly, L., and M. Chesney-Lind. "Feminism and Criminology." *Justice Quarterly.* 5. 1988. pp. 497–438.

Dantzker, M.L. "Higher Education and Policing: Its Effect on the Perception of Job Satisfaction among Police Officers." In N. Ali-Jackson (ed.), *Contemporary Issues in Criminal Justice: Shaping Tomorrow's Systems.* New York: McGraw-Hill. 1995. pp. 104–122.

———. "Identifying Determinants of Job Satisfaction among Police Officers. *Journal of Police and Criminal Psychology.* 10 (1). 1994. pp. 47–56.

———. "Designing a Measure of Job Satisfaction for Policing. *Journal of Crime and Justice.* 16 (2). 1993a. pp. 171–181.

———. "An Issue for Policing—Educational Level and Job Satisfaction: A Research Note." *American Journal of Police.* 12 (2). 1993b. pp. 101–118.

Dantzker, M.L., and B. Kubin. "Job Satisfaction: The Gender Perspective Among Police Officers." *American Journal of Criminal Justice.* 23 (1). 1998. pp. 20–31.

Dantzker, M.L., and M.A. Surette. "Perceived Levels of Job Satisfaction among Police Officers: A Descriptive Review." *Journal of Police and Criminal Psychology.* 11 (2). 1996. pp. 7–12.

Delong, R.K. *An Analysis of Police Perceptions of Community Policing and Female Officers.* Dissertation. Western Michigan University. 1997.

DeLucia, R.C., and T.J. Doyle. *Career Planning in Criminal Justice, Third Edition.* Cincinnati, OH: Anderson Publishing Co. 1998.

DeWine, S., and D. Casbolt. "Networking: External Communications Systems for Female Organizational Members." *Journal of Business Communication.* 20 (2). 1983. pp. 57–67.

Dion, K., and R. Schuller. "Ms. and the Manager: A Tale of Two Stereotypes." *Sex Roles.* 9 (10). 1990. pp. 569–577.

Dobbins, G., W. Long, E. Dedrick, and T. Clemons. "The Role of Self-Monitoring and Gender in Leader Emergence: A Laboratory Field Study." *Journal of Management.* 16 (1). pp. 609–618.

Donnell, S., and J. Hall. "Men and Women As Managers: A Significant Case of No Significant Differences." *Organizational Dynamics.* 8. 1980. pp. 60–77.

Douvan, E. "The Role of Models in Women's Professional Development." *Psychology of Women Quarterly.* 1. pp. 5–20.

Duff, C.S. *Learning from Other Women.* New York: AMACOM. 1999.

Ellison, K.W., and J. Genz. "The Police Officer as Burned-Out Samaritan." *FBI Law Enforcement Bulletin.* 47. 1978. pp. 1–7.

———. *Stress and the Police Officer.* Springfield, IL: Thomas. 1983.

Ely, R. "The Effects of Organizational Demographics and Social Identity on Relationships Among Professional Women." *Administrative Science Quarterly*. 39. 1994. pp. 203–238.

Epstein, C.F. *Deceptive Distinctions: Sex, Gender, and the Social Order.* New York: Russell Sage Foundation. 1988.

——. "Encountering the Male Establishment: Sex-Status Limits on Women's Careers in the Professions." In R.M. Pavalko (ed.), *Sociological Perspectives on Occupations.* Itasca, IL: Peacock. 1972. pp. 364–381.

Etzion, D., and A. Pines. *Sex and Culture as Factors Explaining Reported Coping Behavior and Burnout of Human Service Professionals: A Social Psychological Perspective.* Tel Aviv: Israel Institute of Business Research, Tel Aviv University. 1981.

European Network of Policewomen. *Facts, Figures and General Information.* The Netherlands: European Network of Policewomen. 2000.

Feinman, C. "Women in Law Enforcement." In C. Feinman (ed.), *Women in the Criminal Justice System, Second Edition.* New York: Praeger. 1986. pp. 108–129.

Felkenes, G.T., and J.R. Schroedel. "A Case Study of Minority Women in Policing." *Women and Criminal Justice.* 4. 1993. pp. 65–87.

Fischer, R.J., and G. Green. *Introduction to Security, Sixth Edition.* Boston: Butterworth-Heinemann. 1998.

Fletcher, C. *Breaking and Entering: Women Cops Talk about Life in the Ultimate Men's Club.* New York: Harper Collins. 1995.

Forbes, J., J. Piercy, and T. Hayes. "Women Executives: Breaking Down Barriers?" *Business Horizons.* Nov./Dec. 1998. pp. 6–9.

Gaines, L.K., V.E. Kappeler, and J.B. Vaughn. *Policing in America, Third Edition.* Cincinnati, OH: Anderson Publishing Co. 1999.

Gallery, S.M. (ed.). *Security Management: Readings from Security Management Magazine.* Boston: Butterworth-Heinemann. 1984.

Gomez-Preston, C., and J. Trescott. "Over the Edge: One Police Woman's Story of Emotional and Sexual Harassment." In B.R. Price and N.J. Sokoloff (eds.), *The Criminal Justice System and Women: Offenders, Victims, and Workers, Second Edition.* New York: McGraw-Hill. 1995.

Goolkasian, G.A., R.W. Geddes, and W. DeJong. *Coping with Police Stress.* Washington, DC: U.S. Government Printing Office. 1985.

Gossett, J.L., and J.E. Williams. "Perceived Discrimination Among Women in Law Enforcement." *Women & Criminal Justice.* 10 (1). 1998. pp. 53–73.

Grant, N.K., C. Garrison, and K. McCormick. "Perceived Utilization, Job Satisfaction and Advancement of Police Women." *Public Personnel Management.* 19 (2). 1990. pp. 147–154.

Greenglass, E.R. "Psychological Implications of Sex Bias in the Workplace." *Academic Psychology Bulletin.* 7. 1995. pp. 227–240.

Haar, R.N. "Patterns of Interaction in a Police Patrol Bureau: Race and Gender Barriers to Integration." *Justice Quarterly.* 14 (1). March 1997. pp. 53–85.

Haar, R.N., and M. Morash. "Gender, Race, and Strategies of Coping with Occupational Stress in Policing." *Justice Quarterly.* 16 (2). June 1999. pp. 303–336.

Hale, D.C. "Women in Policing." In G.W. Cordner and D.C. Hale (eds.), *What Works in Policing? Operations and Administration Examined.* 1992. pp. 125–141.

Hale, D.C., and C.L. Bennett. "Realities of Women in Policing." In A. Merlo and J. Pollock (eds.), *Women, Law and Social Control.* Boston: Allyn and Bacon. 1995. pp. 41–54.

Hale, D.C., and D.J. Menniti. "Discrimination and Harassment: Litigation by Women in Policing." In R. Muraskin and T. Alleman (eds.), *It's A Crime: Women and Justice.* Englewood Cliffs, NJ: Regents/Prentice Hall. 1993. pp. 177–189.

Hale, D.C., and S.M. Wyland. "Dragons and Dinosaurs: The Plight of Patrol Women." *Police Forum.* 3. 1993. pp. 1–8.

Harr, J.S., and K.M. Hess. *Seeking Employment in Law Enforcement, Private Security, and Related Fields.* St. Paul, MN: West Publishing Co. 1992.

Harrimann, A. *Women/Men/Management* (2nd ed.) 1996. Westport, CT: Praeger.

Hartmann, H. "Capitalism, Patriarchy, and Job Segregation." Part 2. *Signs.* 1. 1976. pp. 137–169.

Heidensohn, F. *Women in Control? The Role of Women in Law Enforcement.* New York: Oxford University Press. 1992.

Heim, P. *Hardball for Women: Winning at the Game of Business.* New York: Plume. 1993.

Helgesen, S. *The Female Advantage: Women's Ways of Leadership.* New York: Currency Doubleday. 1995.

Helgesen, S. *The Web of Inclusion.* New York: Currency Doubleday. 1995.

Hennig, M., and A. Jardim. *The Managerial Woman.* New York: Anchor Books/Doubleday. 1977.

Hess, K.M., and H.M. Wrobleski. *Introduction to Private Security, Third Edition.* St. Paul: West Publishing Co. 1992.

Hickman, K.G. "Measuring Job Performance Success for Female Officers of the Los Angeles Police Department." Unpublished Doctoral Dissertation. Claremont Graduate School. Los Angeles. 1983.

Higgins, L. "Historical Background of Policewomen's Service." *Journal of Criminal Law, Criminology and Police Science.* 41. 1951. pp. 822–833.

Hindman, R.E. "A Survey Related to Use of Female Law Enforcement Officers." *Police Chief.* 42 (4). 1975. pp. 58–60.

Horne, P. *Women in Law Enforcement.* Springfield, IL: Charles C. Thomas. 1980.

Hughes, E.C. "Dilemmas and Contradictions of Status." *American Journal of Sociology.* 50. 1944. pp. 353–359.

Hunt, J. "The Development of Rapport Through Negotiation of Gender in Field Work Among Police." *Human Organization.* 43. 1984. pp. 283–296.

———. "The Logic of Sexism Among Police." *Women and Criminal Justice.* 1. 1990. pp. 3–30.

Hutzel, E. *The Policewomen's Handbook.* New York: Columbia University Press. 1933.

International Association of Chiefs of Police. *The Future of Women in Policing: Mandates for Action.* Alexandria, VA: IACP. 1998.

International Association of Women Police (2001, Feb. 4—last updated). [Homepage of International Association of Women Police], [Online]. Available: http://www.iapi.org/index.htm [2001, February 4].

Johnson, P. "Women and Power: Toward a Theory of Effectiveness." *Journal of Social Issues.* 32 (3). 1976. pp. 99–110.

Jurik, N.C. "An Officer and a Lady: Organizational Barriers to Women Working as Correctional Officers in Men's Prisons." *Social Problems.* 32. 1985. pp. 375–388.

———. "Striking a Balance: Female Correctional Officers, Gender Role Stereotypes, and Male Prisons." *Sociological Inquiry.* 58. 1988. pp. 291–305.

Jurik, N.C., and G.J. Halemba. "Gender, Working Conditions, and the Job Satisfaction of Women in a Nontraditional Occupation: Female Correctional Officers in Men's Prisons." *The Sociological Quarterly.* 25. 1984. pp. 551–566.

Kakalik, J.S., and S. Wildhorn. *The Private Police Industry: Its Nature and Extent.* Santa Monica, CA: The Rand Corporation. 1971.

Kanter, R.M. "The Impact of Hierarchical Structures on the Work Behavior of Women and Men." *Sociological Problems.* 23. 1976. pp. 415–430.

———. *Men and Women of the Corporation.* New York: Basic Books. 1977.

———. "The Impact of Hierarchal Structures on the Work Behavior of Women and Men." *Social Problems.* 23. 1976. pp. 415–430.

Kanter, R.M., and B.A. Stein (eds.). *Life in Organizations.* New York: Basic Books. 1979.

Karsten, M.F. *Management and Gender: Issues and Attitudes.* Westport, CT: Quorum Books. 1994.

Kizziah, C., and M. Morris. *Evaluation of Women in Policing Program: Newton, Massachusetts.* Oakland, CA: Approach Associates. 1977.

Kram, K. "Phases of the Mentor Relationship." *Academy of Management Journal.* 26. 1983. pp. 608–625.

Kram, K., and D. Hall. "Mentoring as an Antidote to Stress During Corporate Trauma." *Human Resource Management.* 28. 1983. pp. 493–510.

Kram, K., and V. Parker. "Women Mentoring Women Creating Conditions for Connection." *Business Horizons.* March/April 1993. pp. 42–51.

Kranda, A. "Women in Policing: The Importance of Mentoring." *The Police Chief.* October 1998.

Kraska, P.B., and V.E. Kappeler. "To Serve and Pursue: Exploring Police Sexual Violence against Women." *Justice Quarterly.* 12. 1995. pp. 85–111.

Lafontaine, E., and L. Tredeau. "The Frequency, Sources, and Correlates of Sexual Harassment Among Women in Traditional Male Occupations." *Sex Roles.* 15. 1986. pp. 433–442.

Laws, J.L. "The Psychology of Tokenism: An Analysis." *Sex Roles.* 1. 1975. pp. 209–223.

Leger, K. "Public Perceptions of Female Police Officers on Patrol." *American Journal of Criminal Justice.* 21 (2). 1997. pp. 231–249.

Lersch, K.M. "Exploring Gender Differences in Citizen Allegations of Misconduct: An Analysis of a Municipal Police Department." *Women & Criminal Justice.* 9 (4). 1998. pp. 69–79.

Linden, R. "Women in Policing: A Study of Lower Mainland Royal Canadian Mounted Police Detachments. *Canadian Police College Journal.* 7. 1983. pp. 217–229.

Lunnenborg, P.W. *Women Police Officers: Current Career Profile.* Springfield, IL: Charles C. Thomas Publisher. 1989.

Lykes, M.B. "Discrimination and Coping in the Lives of Black Women: Analysis of Oral History Data." *Journal of Social Issues.* 39. 1983. pp. 79–100.

Manning, P.K. "Police Occupational Culture: Segmentation, Politics, and Sentiments." Unpublished manuscript. Michigan State University, School of Criminal Justice. 1994.

——. "Toward a Theory of Police Organization: Polarities and Change." Unpublished manuscript. Michigan State University, School of Criminal Justice. 1993.

Mariette, C. "Androgynous Management." *Women Police.* 22. 1988. pp. 6–7.

Martin, S. "*Police*women and Police*women*: Occupational Role Dilemmas and Choices of Female Officers." *Journal of Police Science and Administration.* 7. 1979. pp. 314–323.

Martin, S.E. *"Breaking and Entering": Policewomen on Patrol.* Berkeley: University of California Press, 1980.

———. *On the Move: The Status of Women in Policing.* Washington, DC: Police Foundation. 1990b.

———. "The Effectiveness of Affirmative Action: The Case of Women in Policing." *Justice Quarterly.* 8. 1991. pp. 489–504.

———. "The Changing Status of Women Officers: Gender and Power in Police Work." In I.L. Moyers (ed.), *The Changing Role of Women in the Criminal Justice System.* Prospect Heights, IL: Waveland. 1992. pp. 281–305.

———. " 'Outsider Within' the Station House: The Impact of Race and Gender on Black Women Police." *Social Problems.* 41. 1994. pp. 383–400.

———. "The Interactive Effects of Race and Sex on Women Police Officers." In B.R. Price and J.J. Sokoloff (eds.), *The Criminal Justice System and Women: Offenders, Victims, and Workers.* New York: McGraw-Hill. 1995. pp. 383–397.

———. "Women Officers on the Move: An Update on Women in Policing." In R.G. Dunham and G.P. Alpert (eds.), *Critical Issues in Policing: Contemporary Readings.* Prospect Heights, IL: Waveland Press. 5. 1997. pp. 363–384.

Martin, S.E., and N.C. Jurik. *Doing Justice, Doing Gender: Women in Law and Criminal Justice Occupations.* Thousand Oaks, CA: Sage Publications. 1996.

Massengill, D., and N. DiMarco. "Sex-role Stereotypes and Requisite Management Characteristics: A Current Replication." *Sex Roles.* 5. 1979. pp. 561–570.

Milgram, D. *Personal Interview.* Washington, D.C. 1999.

Miller, S.L. *Gender and Community Policing: Walking the Talk.* Boston: Northeastern University Press. 1999.

Milton, C. *Women in Policing.* Washington, DC: Police Foundation. 1972.

Mintzberg, H. *The Nature of Managerial Work.* New York: Harper and Row. 1973.

Moore, L., and A. Rickel. "Characteristics of Women in Traditional and Nontraditional Managerial Roles." *Personnel Psychology.* 33. 1980. pp. 317–333.

Morash, M., and R.N. Haar. "Gender, Workplace Problems, and Stress in Policing." *Justice Quarterly.* 12 (1). 1995. pp. 113–136.

Morash, M., and J. Greene. "Evaluating Women on Patrol: A Critique of Contemporary Wisdom." *Evaluation Review.* 10. 1986. pp. 230–255.

More, H.W. *Special Topics in Policing, Second Edition.* Cincinnati: Anderson Publishing Co. 1998.

Morris, A. *Women, Crime and Criminal Justice.* New York: Basil Blackwell. 1987.

Morton, J. (ed.) *Change, Challenge, and Choices: Women's Role in Modern Corrections.* Laurel, MD: American Correctional Association. 1991.

Myers, G.E. *A Municipal Mother: Portland's Lola Greene Baldwin, America's First Policewoman.* Corvallis, OR: Oregon State University Press. 1995.

National Center for Women and Policing. *Equality Denied: The Status of Women in Policing 1999.* Los Angeles, CA: National Center for Women and Policing. 2000.

National Center for Women and Policing. *Equality Denied: The Status of Women in Policing 2000.* Los Angeles, CA: National Center for Women and Policing. 2001.

Neighbors, H.W., J. Jackson, P. Bowman, and G. Gurin. "Stress, Coping, and Black Mental Health: Preliminary Findings from a National Study." *Prevention in Human Services.* 2. 1983. pp. 5–29.

Ott, M.E. "Effects of the Male-Female Ratio at Work: Policewomen and Male Nurses." *Psychology of Women Quarterly.* 13. 1989. pp. 41–57.

Pendergrass, V.E., and N.M. Ostrove. "A Survey of Stress in Women in Policing." *Journal of Police Science Administration.* 12. 1984. pp. 303–309.

Pennsylvania State Police. *Pennsylvania State Police Female Trooper Study.* Harrisburg, PA: Author. 1974.

Peters, T. *The Circle of Innovation: You Can't Shrink Your Way to Greatness.* New York: Vintage Books. 1999.

Peters, T. *The Pursuit of Wow!* New York: Vintage Books. 1994.

Pike, D.L. "Women in Police Academy Training: Some Aspects of Organizational Response." In I. Moyer (ed.), *Changing Roles of Women in the Criminal Justice System: Offenders, Victims, and Professionals, Second Edition.* pp. 261–280. Prospect Heights, IL. Waveland. 1992.

Plummer, D.L., and S. Slane. "Patterns of Coping in Racially Stressful Situations." *Journal of Black Psychology.* 22. 1996. pp. 302–315.

Polisar, J., and D. Milgram. "Recruiting, Integrating and Retaining Women Police Officers: Strategies That Work." *Police Chief.* Oct. 1988. pp. 42–50.

Poole, E.D., and M.R. Pogrebin. "Factors Affecting the Decision to Remain in Policing: A Study of Women Officers." *Journal of Police Science and Administration.* 14 (1). 1988. pp. 49–55.

Price, B.R. "A Study of Leadership Strength of Female Police Executives." *Journal of Police Science and Administration.* 2. pp. 219–226.

Price, B.R., and S. Gavin. "A Century of Women in Policing." In B.R. Price and N.J. Sokoloff (eds.), *The Criminal Justice System and Women.* New York: Clark Boardman. 1982. pp. 399–412.

Raven, B.H. "Social Influence and Power." In I.D. Steiner and M. Fishbein (eds.), *Current Studies in Social Psychology*. 1965. pp. 371–382.

Reaves, B.A., and A.L. Goldberg. *Law Enforcement Management and Administrative Statistics, 1997: Data for Individual State and Local Agencies with 100 or More Officers*. U.S. Department of Justice. Bureau of Justice Statistics. April 1999.

Remmington, P.W. "Women in the Police: Integration or Separation?" *Qualitative Sociology*. 6 (6). 1983. pp. 118–135.

Reskin, B.F., and P.A. Roos. *Job Queues, Gender Queues: Explaining Women's Inroads into Male Occupations*. Philadelphia: Temple University Press. 1990.

Roche, G.R. "Much Ado About Mentors." *Business Review*. 57. 1979. pp. 14–28.

Rosen, B., and T. Jardee. "Perceived Sex Differences in Managerially Relevant Characteristics. *Sex Roles*. 4. 1978. pp. 837–843.

Rosener, J. "Ways Women Lead." *Harvard Business Review*. 68 (6). 1990. pp. 119–145.

Rubenstein, J. *City Police*. New York: Farrar, Straus, and Giroux. 1972.

Rutland, C.M. "Comparative Analysis of the Relationship Between Social Background Factors and Training Performance of Male and Female Security Specialists." Master's Thesis. California State University, Sacramento. 1978.

Scarborough, K.E., P.A. Collins, C. Shain, and A. Cordner. "Women Officers' Perception of Networking and Mentoring in Policing." Paper presentation. Annual meeting of the Academy of Criminal Justice Sciences. New Orleans, LA. March 2000.

Scarborough K.E., and C. Hemmens. "Women Defendants in Law Enforcement Civil Liability Cases." Paper presentation. Annual meeting of the Academy of Criminal Justice Sciences. Albuquerque, NM. March 1998.

Schatzman, L., and A. Strauss. *Field Research: Strategies for a Natural Sociology*. Englewood Cliffs, NJ: Prentice-Hall. 1973.

Schein, V.E. "Power, Sex and Systems." *Women in Management Review*. 9 (1). 1994. p. 4.

Schulz, D.M. "Invisible No More: A Social History of Women in U.S. Policing." In B.R. Price and N.J. Sokoloff (eds.), *The Criminal Justice System and Women: Offenders, Victims and Workers*, New York: McGraw-Hill, Inc. 1995.

Schulz, D.M. *From Social Worker to Crimefighter: Women in United States Municipal Policing*. London: Praeger. 1995.

Seagram, B.C., and C. Stark-Adamac. "Women in Canadian Urban Policing: Why Are They Leaving Us?" *The Police Chief*. 54 (10). 1992. pp. 120–128.

Sherman, L.J. "An Evaluation of Policewomen on Patrol in a Suburban Police Department. *Journal of Police Science and Administration*. 3 (4). 1975. pp. 434–438.

Sichel, J.L., L.N. Friedman, J.C. Quint, and M.E. Smith. *Women on Patrol: A Pilot Study of Police Performance in New York City*. Washington, DC: National Institute of Law Enforcement and Criminal Justice. 1977.

Silbert, M.H. "Job Stress and Burnout of New Police Officer." *Police Chief*. 49 (6). 1982. pp. 46–68.

Sinetar, M. *The Mentor's Spirit*. New York: St. Martin's/Griffin. 1998.

Skolnick, J. *Justice without Trial: Law Enforcement in a Democratic Society*. New York: Wiley. 1966.

Smith, P.B., and M.H. Bond. *Social Psychology Across Cultures, Second Edition*. London: Prentice-Hall. 1993.

Snortum, J.R., and J.C. Beyers. "Patrol Activities of Male and Female Officers as a Function of Work Experience." *Police Studies*. 6. 1983. pp. 36–42.

Staines, G., C. Tavris, and T.E. Jayaratne. "The Queen Bee Syndrome." *Psychology Today*. Jan. 1974. pp. 55–58, 60.

Stanley, L., and S. Wise. *Breaking Out: Feminist Consciousness and Feminist Research*. London: Rutledge and Kegal Paul. 1983.

Stickley, A.V. "Women Supervising Men." *Women Police*. 21. December 1987. p. 9.

Stroman, C.A., and R. Seltzer. "Racial Differences in Coping with Job Stress: A Research Note." *Journal of Social Behavior and Personality*. 66. 1991. pp. 309–318.

Stromberg, A.H., and S. Harkess. *Working Women: Theories and Facts in Perspective* (2nd Edition). Mountain View, CA: Mayfield Publishing Company. 1988.

Thomann, D.A., and T. Serritella. "Preventing Sexual Harassment in Law Enforcement Agencies." *The Police Chief*. September 1994. pp. 31–35.

Thorne, B. *Gender Play: Girls and Boys in School*. New Brunswick, NJ: Rutgers University Press. 1994.

Vega, M., and I.J. Silverman. "Female Police Officers as Viewed by their Male Counterparts." *Police Studies*. 5. 1982. pp. 31–39.

www.asisonline.org/profdev.html *ASIS Professional Development Web Page*.

www.ssrgroup.com/page/workbook.htm *Calling All Women—Who Me?* pp. 1–2. 5/22/99.

Walker, S. *A Critical History of Police Reform*. Lexington: Lexington Books. 1977.

Walsh, W.F. "Private/Public Police Stereotypes: A Different Perspective." *Security Journal*. 1. 1989. pp. 21–27.

Wertsch, T.L. "Walking the Thin Blue Line: Policewomen and Tokenism Today." *Women and Criminal Justice*. 9 (3). 1998. pp. 23–61.

Westley, W. *Violence and the Police: A Sociological Study of Law, Custom, and Morality*. Cambridge, MA: MIT Press. 1970.

Wexler, J.G. "Role Styles of Women Police Officers." *Sex Roles*. 12. 1985. pp. 749–755.

Wexler, J.G., and D.D. Logan. "Sources of Stress Among Women Police Officers." *Journal of Police Science and Administration*. 13. 1983. pp. 98–105.

White, S.E., and K.E. Marino. "Job Attitudes and Police Stress: An Exploratory Study of Causation." *Journal of Police and Administration*. 11. 1983. pp. 264–274.

Williams, C.L. *Gender Differences at Work: Women and Men in Nontraditional Occupations*. Berkeley, CA: University of California Press. 1989.

Wilson, N.K. "Women in the Criminal Justice Professions: An Analysis of Status Conflict." In N.H. Rafter and E.A. Stanko (eds.), *Judge, Lawyer, Victim, Thief*. Stoughton, MA: Northeastern University Press. 1982. pp. 359–374.

Worden, A.P. "The Attitudes of Women and Men in Policing: Testing Conventional and Contemporary Wisdom." *Criminology*. 31. 1993. pp. 203–242.

Yoder, J. "Rethinking Tokenism: Looking Beyond Numbers." *Gender and Society*. 5 (2). 1991. pp. 178–192.

Yoder, J., J. Adams, S. Grove, and R. Priest. *Psychology of Women Quarterly*. 9 (1). 1985. pp. 119–131.

Young, C.J., D.L. Mackenzie, and C.W. Sherif. "In Search of Token Women in Academia." *Psychology of Women Quarterly*. 4. 1980. pp. 508–525.

Young, M. *An Inside Job: Policing and Police Culture in Britain*. Oxford: Clarendon. 1991.

Zhao, J., Q. Thurman, and N. He. "Sources of Job Satisfaction Among Police Officers: A Test of Demographic and Work Environment Models." *Justice Quarterly*. 16 (1). March 1999. pp. 153–173.

Zimmer, L.E. *Women Guarding Men*. Chicago: University of Chicago Press. 1986.

Zupan, L.L. "Gender-related Differences in Correctional Officers' Perceptions and Attitudes." *Journal of Criminal Justice*. 14. 1986. pp. 349–361.

Index